ZEN

Simply Sitting

ZEN
Simply Sitting

a Zen monk's commentary on the *Fukanzazengi*
~ Universal Guide to the Practice of Zazen ~
by Master Dogen (1200 – 1253)

commentaries by
Rei Ryu Philippe Coupey

translated from the French
by Marc Shaver and Elaine Konopka

HOHM PRESS
Prescott, Arizona

Cover design: Kim Johansen
Layout and design: Zachary Parker
Cover photo by Juliette Heymann

Library of Congress Cataloging-in-Publication Data

Coupey, Philippe.
    Zen, simply sitting : a Zen monk's commentary on the Fukanzazengi,
universal guide to the practice of zazen by Master Dogen (1200 - 1253) /
commentaries by Rei Ryu Philippe Coupey ; translated from the French by Marc Shaver
and Elaine Konopka.
        p. cm.
    Includes bibliographical references and index.
    ISBN 1-890772-61-5 (pbk. : alk. paper)
    1. Dogen, 1200-1253. Fukan zazengi. 2. Meditation--Zen Buddhism. 3.
Sotoshu--Doctrines. I. Dogen, 1200-1253. Fukan zazengi. English. II. Title.
III. Title: Universal guide to the practice of zazen by Master Dogen (1200-1253).
    BQ9449.D654F8433 2006
    294.3'4435--dc22
                                        2006023711

HOHM PRESS
P.O. Box 2501
Prescott, Arizona 86302
800-381-2700
www.hohmpress.com

This book was printed in the U.S.A. on recycled, acid-free paper using soy ink.

10 09 08 07 06   1 2 3 4 5

I dedicate this book to my master, Taisen Deshimaru.

I wish to thank
the Great Disperser of Illusions, my friend Lee Lozowick,
and his very fine editor Regina Sara Ryan;
my disciples Paul Buller, Guy Faure, Elaine Konopka,
and Jean-Pierre Romain for their invaluable help;
Reverend Shohaku Okumura;
and the Association Zen Sans Demeure
for its generous support.

Zen is the confrontation with your innermost self,
with what you have in your guts.
The first years are easy.
Five years – piece of cake.
Ten years is a little harder.
After fifteen or twenty years it's not easy at all.
In fact, you have to be more careful then,
because the path becomes more and more perilous....
This is the highest of spiritual quests,
and if it's easy, then it's not authentic.

— Philippe Coupey

CONTENTS

FOREWORD

How refreshing! In these times of the tragic dumbing-down of
the true teaching, in these times of foppish and confused self-
centeredness, in these times of the rejection of even the slightest desire to see-clearly and live on the basis of such clarity, and,
exactly relevant to the book you are hopefully about to read, in
these times of the so-called modernization of Buddhism, in all
its forms, said modernization merely being a justification for
a comprehensive rejection of anything that would serve our
stream-entering vow to Realize, to animate Truth, to find great
Satori or Buddha-Mind and realize that there was nothing to
seek for and no separation to begin with, yes, in such times, how
totally refreshing to read a commentary that does not fall into
the above mentioned pathologies.

You all know, beyond a shadow of a doubt, that we live in
dark times, times in which we suspect everything, the mature
guide, the love of a devoted partner, the reality of God, or Buddha, if you prefer, the possibility of the pure, pristine stainless
Being as none other than ourselves. You all know, and I am sure
of it, know in your deepest secret heart-of-hearts, that we, in our
so called "post-modern" world (whatever *that* means?!) that our

reliance upon, even addiction to, the technology of a faith-less, scientific machine, is the path to untold suffering, is in fact a landscape so bleak that we could die of starvation, and in fact will, no matter how much we had to eat or drink.

Sir Buddha gave us a Way, a path to lead us "from darkness to light" as the Hindu Scriptures say. And what are we doing with this gift? We are desecrating it with an unwillingness to practice according to His instruction. We define practice based on whatever comforts and self-indulgences we feel like in any given moment. But here, in your hands, you hold a commentary that tells the truth, in the face of an overwhelming contemporary "Buddhist scene" that does not want to hear the truth, that has forgotten truth in its headlong rush to compromise once noble ideals in the wish to serve "everyman," in other words the lowest common denominator of consciousness.

All of the great Realizers, in all of the great Traditions, have always pointed us towards the highest denominator, which has always been far from common. They have pointed us there with their dharma, their writing, prose and poetry, their painting and sculpture, their archery, Ikebana, calligraphy, Tea Ceremony, their way of dress, ways of speech, way of being, and especially through their active engagement in life. They have left us countless exemplary demonstrations of a willingness to sacrifice everything and to compromise nothing, to Realize this great Way. And also, today, we tout these Realizers as old-fashioned has-beens who may have had relevance in their time and place, but can't speak to us, us here in the 21st century. Reverend Ike, a flamboyant and eloquent orator, once said, "There's nothing as bad as a good excuse and the better the excuse, the worse it is." And it is bad these days. Bad in the world and bad on the so called path in what could and should be a constantly revitalized and revitalizing field of truth but has become, these days, barely little more than a glorified spiritualized spa, offering harmony and health through self-glorying programs in posing, vanity and pride.

And here comes Philippe Coupey's blunt, clear, striking commentary on the *Fukanzazengi* to shake up the sloth and the trance of most of today's Buddhists. Dogen's work was first written in the 13th century and it is as relevant today as ever it was. One can only shout Hallelujah – oh, oops, sorry. I mean one can only offer a profound and grateful *katzu* and a deep *gassho* for his work, small in size but very large in impact, so vitally crucial in these times, times in which the brilliant sun of Dharma has been obscured by the clouds of illusion and ego is already counting the spoils of its victory. But wait! It isn't entirely too late, as this thin volume makes evident. There are still those few who know the sun shines brightly above those clouds and who are passionately extolling the actuality of the existence of this sun. Whack me with that stick and wake me up! Hey, hey, hey you, yes, you who still want the true teaching, the raw (but not un-cooked) and radiant practice of this, here, now, as-it-is. Here it is, at least here it will be when you finish this blustering introduction and get to the heart and bones and flesh, the meat of this book, M. Coupey's commentary, educed from his own long, long road of practice with his extraordinary master, Taisen Deshimaru.

A quote from a 20th-century Indian Master, Meher Baba: "Realization is for heroes who, while the knife is slashing their throats, take pleasure in the pain of dying." Well, the implication being that realization is not for those whose fascination and distraction lies in the seduction of a coffee in one hand and their dick (men or women) in the other. Is their anything wrong with coffee or sex? Hell no! Bring 'em on, and, when "coffee" and "sex" are what has captured us and holds us captive, imprisoned in our inability to make an adult and free choice, then we have bought into the demand to lose all courage, to forego dignity, nobility and elegance in life, for the wages of morbid self-reference, Narcissuses all, staring at our own navels and wishing we were someone else, something else, anything but THIS. Ah, despair.

So read, read this most wonderful instruction, the *Fukanzazengi* of Dogen and the commentary of Coupey, informed by Deshimaru, and weep, as they say in poker when the winning hand is lain down, read 'em and weep. In this case weep for the demise of confusion and mis-interpretation, for the death of projection and editorializing, opinionating and expectation. Weep, but not too long, for life is waiting to spill over with its joy, with its sorrow, with all of its infinite facets, with its bursting, juicy THIS, here, now, as-it-is. And, having written way too much and pompously preached pretty pontifically, I leave you with Dogen's own plea:

> I beseech you, honored disciples of Zen, long accustomed to feeling for the elephant in the dark, do not fear the true dragon. Devote your energies to the Way which points to the absolute without detour. Respect the realized man who is situated beyond the actions of men...your treasure house will open of itself, and you can use it as you wish.

– lee lozowick
Prescott, Arizona
January 21, 2006

Translator's Preface

Direct heart-to-heart transmission from one human being to another over the centuries, across borders, seas and mountains, leveling differences of language, race, culture and social condition, is the mark of Zen tradition over time. The writings of the masters are only shadows of their whole teaching.

This book presents an English translation of Master Philippe Coupey's commentaries on the *Fukanzazengi*, one of the founding texts of the Soto School, written in 13th-century Japan by Master Dogen, who, returning from China, was beginning his life's work of transmission.

Dogen, if he had only written (and he did write a great deal), would not have been an authentic Zen master. And Coupey, if he only produced commentaries on Zen texts, would simply be a student, or scholar, of those texts.

Zen teaching is elsewhere. Its words are more often spoken than written. The present commentaries, for example, were first given as *kusen* (oral teaching) in the Paris Zen Dojo. They were meant to be heard directly by those present as part of the living experience of zazen. The kusen is an innovation in Zen teaching which was used by Kodo Sawaki in Japan and developed in Europe by Taisen Deshimaru. Although innovation is not particularly sought after or encouraged in Zen, the kusen has proven to be a powerful teaching tool that respects the traditional values. We might say that it is a conservative innovation. Ink and paper suffice for the expression of ideas, and this book can only do what books can do. The reader is asked to bear in mind the particular context in which these words were pronounced.

But Zen teaching, of course, is more than what is said. It opens, unfolds, in silence as much as in speech, or more so. Gestures, gazes, exemplary behavior are as central as discourse. Those who have the good fortune to practice regularly with Coupey are invariably struck by his sincerity, intuition and natural authority, and by the bite of his *kyosaku*. Manner and matter form a whole, and it is difficult to reduce a master's teaching to a text.

But all the rest would be merely anecdotal without the reality of Zen practice. The zazen posture itself is the center and the periphery, that one thing needful, without which Zen tradition would rapidly become frivolous, theatrical, hollow.

We ask a lot of the reader. Having now explained that this text is possibly the least important element of Coupey's teaching, we nevertheless recommend it without hesitation as an introduction to the depth and the sound of that teaching and as an excellent companion to Dogen's *Fukanzazengi*.

– Marc Shaver

Author's Preface

The *Fukanzazengi* is the first text that Master Dogen wrote when he returned to his native Japan after spending five years in China. He wanted very much to teach what his master, Nyojo, had passed on to him. For it was through Nyojo that Dogen was linked to the direct transmission from Bodhidharma and Shakyamuni Buddha. There may be no other text that has so deeply influenced not only the Soto Zen lineage, but the entire world.

This is Dogen's main text on how to do zazen. Two of his later works, the *Bendowa* and the *Genjokoan*, explain and expand upon this early text. In fact, I believe that every one of the ninety-five chapters of the *Shobogenzo* can be read as an explanation of the *Fukanzazengi*.

Fukan means "recommended for the people" – guidelines not just for priests and monks but for lay people as well; *zazen* is seated meditation; *gi* is a law, principle, or practice. So *Fukanzazengi* is the "Universal Guide to the Practice of Zazen." It is not a long text, but it is an essential one for both beginners and experienced practitioners. It is venerated in our Zen tradition and recited in all Soto temples. I think that every person who does zazen should know this text – not necessarily by heart, the way the Japanese do, but by thoroughly understanding its meaning.

Master Deshimaru once said, "For more than forty years I have read and reread the *Fukanzazengi* every day, morning and evening, before and after zazen, and even sometimes without doing zazen." We often hear it said that it is not necessary to study the sutras, to fill our heads with studying the Way. That may be true for those who have already read these texts. But for those who have not studied, yet continue with zazen, it would be a pity not to go further. If you practice alone, it is especially important to study a text like the *Fukanzazengi* before or after zazen. Because if you're alone it is easy to lose the way, to pile up more and more karma, instead of cutting it off with the help of a guide or a master.

The *Fukanzazengi* was first written by Master Dogen in 1227, re-copied by his own hand in 1233, and then rewritten and put into its final form in 1242 or 1243 when he had fully matured and was approaching the last part of his life. There are, therefore, two versions of the text: the earlier one, called the *Tenpukubon*, and the later, the *Rufubon*. It is interesting to note the differences between them. For example, in the earlier version Dogen speaks of *samadhi* – the highest form of concentration – as a means to obtaining satori. Later in his life, he deleted this notion and instead strongly emphasized the idea that practice and satori are one and the same (*shu sho ichi nyo*). This way of looking at things probably comes easier with age, as the end of your life draws near. Not only do you have less to lose, but you also have less to gain. The mind becomes clear.

I have used this final version, the *Rufubon*, as the basis for my commentary.

PART I

Text of the Fukanzazengi

Note to the Reader: Most foreign words are defined in the Glossary at the end of this book.

Fukanzazengi

~ Universal Guide to the Practice of Zazen ~
by Master Dogen (1200 - 1253)

The Way is fundamentally perfect. It penetrates everything. How could it depend on practice and realization? The Dharma vehicle is free and unhindered. What need can there be for the concentrated efforts of men? In truth, the Great Body is well beyond the dust of the world. Who could think it possible to clean it? It is never separate from anyone; it is always exactly where you are. Why go here or there to practice?

However, if there is a separation, be it ever so small, the Way is as distant as the sky from the earth. If even the slightest like or dislike arises, the mind is lost in confusion. Imagine a person who is proud of his understanding, filled with illusions about his own enlightenment, who has barely glimpsed the wisdom that penetrates all things, who has entered the Way and cleared his mind, giving rise to the desire to touch heaven itself. Such a person has begun a preliminary and limited exploration of the outer regions, but he is still not completely on the vital Way of absolute emancipation.

Need I speak of the Buddha, who possessed innate knowledge? We can still feel today the effect of the six years he spent sitting completely still in the lotus posture. And through Bodhidharma the seal of the transmission has come down to us and has preserved the memory of his nine years of meditation in front of a wall. Since it was thus for the saints of old, how could people today dispense with navigating the Way?

You must therefore abandon a practice based on intellectual understanding, running after words, and clinging to the letter. You must learn to turn and direct your light inward to illuminate your true nature. Body and mind will fall away and your original face will appear. If you want to reach thusness, then you must practice thusness without delay.

For *sanzen*, a quiet room is best. Eat and drink moderately. Put aside all engagements and abandon all business. Do not think, "This is good" or "That is bad." Do not take sides for or against. Stop all movement of the conscious mind. Do not judge your thoughts or viewpoints. Do not desire to become a buddha. Zazen has absolutely nothing to do with sitting or lying down.

At the place where you usually sit, spread out a thick mat and place a cushion upon it. Sit either in the lotus or the half-lotus posture. In the lotus posture, first place your right foot on your left thigh, and then your left foot on your right thigh. For the half-lotus, simply place your left foot on your right thigh. Be sure to loosen your belt and your clothing and arrange them properly. Next put your right hand on your left foot and your left hand on your right palm, with the palms turned upward and the tips of your thumbs touching. Sit up straight without leaning to the left or right, forward or backward. Make sure that your ears are lined up with your shoulders, and your nose with your navel. Put your tongue against the front of the palate. The mouth is closed and the teeth touch. Always keep your eyes open and breathe gently through your nose.

When you are in the correct posture, take a deep breath in and out. Swing your body left and right and settle into a steady posture. Think not-thinking. How do you think not-thinking? Beyond thinking – *hishiryo*. This in itself is the essential art of zazen.

The zazen of which I speak is not about learning to meditate. It is none other than the Dharma of peace and happiness, the practice-realization of perfect awakening. Zazen is the manifestation of ultimate reality. Traps and nets can never touch it. When you have touched its heart you are like the dragon entering the sea and the tiger entering the mountains. Understand that at this precise moment the real Dharma is manifested and that, from the beginning, physical and mental weakness and distraction are cast aside.

When you get up, move easily, without haste, calmly and deliberately. Do not stand up suddenly or brusquely. When we look at the past we see that transcending both awakening and non-awakening, dying while sitting or while standing, has always depended on the strength of zazen.

Moreover, it is impossible for the dualistic mind to understand the possibility of enlightenment in the occasion provided by a finger, a flag, a needle, or a mallet, or the attainment of understanding thanks to a *hossu*, a fist, a stick, or a shout. In truth, it cannot be better understood through the use of supernatural powers. It is beyond what human beings can see or hear – is it not a principle which precedes knowledge and perception?

However, it does not matter whether you are intelligent or not. There is no difference between the dull and the sharp-witted. When you concentrate your effort with one-mindedness, that in itself is negotiating the Way. Practice-realization is naturally pure. Going forward is a matter of everyday living.

On the whole, in this world and others, in India and in China, the Buddha seal is respected. The particularity of this school is simply devotion to zazen, sitting still with complete commitment. Although it is said that there are as many minds as there are humans, everyone must practice the Way in the same manner: by practicing zazen. Why give up the place reserved for you at home to wander the dusty realms of other lands? One false step and you stray from the Way that is set out right before you.

You have had the unique chance to take human form. Do not waste your time. You are contributing to the essential work of the Buddha Way. Who could take vain pleasure in the spark from a flint? Form and substance are like dew on the grass, destiny like lightning, vanishing in a flash.

I beseech you, honored disciples of Zen, long accustomed to groping the elephant in the dark: do not fear the true dragon. Devote your energies to the Way which points directly to the absolute. Respect the realized person who is beyond human actions. Harmonize with the enlightenment of the buddhas; succeed to the legitimate dynasty of the patriarchs' satori. Always behave this way, and you will be like them. Your treasure house will open of itself, and you can use it as you wish.

PART II

Commentary on the Text

Chapter One
The Highest Spiritual Quest

*The Way is fundamentally perfect.
It penetrates everything. How could it
depend on practice and realization?*

The *Fukanzazengi* begins with zazen-mind: not-two, non-dualistic, fundamentally perfect (*mo to*, in Japanese).

Then Master Dogen asks us: since the Way is fundamentally perfect, why do we need to practice? Now there's a good question. What he means is, why is it necessary to add anything at all to what is already there? Why add anything to ourselves or to our egos? Why should we try to increase or decrease anything at all? The Way is everywhere, so why go looking for it?

Here we can see the difference between the Zen of masters Dogen and Deshimaru on one hand, and that of the Rinzai School or the Soto-Rinzai mix on the other. The latter says that you have to seek and train constantly in order to obtain satori, while Dogen starts right off at the top of the mountain: there is no progress to be made, no other mountain to be climbed.

That does not mean that there is nothing; it simply means that the mind changes.

The opening of the *Fukanzazengi* reminds me of the thirty-first verse of the *Shinjinmei*, by Master Sosan:

> The substance of the great Way is generous.
> It is neither hard nor easy.

"Generous" here means universal, cosmic, not fixed in one place or time, not even in the here and now. So, naturally, automatically and unconsciously, if we follow the cosmic order, we are on the Way.

The Way is everywhere. The Dharma is everywhere. Buddha nature is everywhere. It is under the feet and over the head of a Zen master, just as it is under the feet and over the head of a killer, in spite of all human reasoning. Even the very worst killer is not cut off from the Dharma. That's the generosity of the great Way, which is neither difficult nor easy. A line from a poem by Wanshi echoes this idea. I use it sometimes as a mantra:

> The entire universe shines and preaches the Dharma.

These first few lines of the *Fukanzazengi* are striking and deep. Dogen is saying that the Way is not dependent on the practice of zazen or on the satori of Buddha or any other master. We often hear the opposite taught in most Buddhist schools. On the other hand, many scholars and intellectuals embrace

Dogen's idea that we don't need to practice to be awakened. Books on Zen written by professors and scholars are often dedicated to Eno, the sixth patriarch. Why? Because Eno said that awakening doesn't depend on zazen, and they like that.

Dogen had certainly heard of the *mondo* between Eno and a monk who asked, "All the Chan masters say that if you want to realize the Way, then you have to practice zazen and *samadhi*. Do you agree?" Eno answered, "The Way depends on the awakening of the mind. How could it depend on zazen?"

People who are impressed by that take it at face value, and their interpretation suits them because it gives them a good reason to do nothing. A long practice is not always easy, especially when you realize that it involves putting up with other people – although great masters do that all their lives.

I have no doubt whatsoever concerning the absolute necessity of sitting in front of a wall with no purpose and no goal. Still, it's not easy to explain what Eno and Dogen mean. The perfection of the Way does not depend on practice or satori because the Way exists within us – not in others, not in something else. I remember a sesshin in Val d'Isère when Master Deshimaru said something similar to this. A Kurdish doctor stood up right in the middle of zazen and shouted, "So why are we sitting here? I'm finished with all this. I'm out of here. I'm not stupid like you!" And he stormed out. That's a very common attitude. The doctor really thought that in order to practice the Way you need to seek out or invent something new. It's just not so.

In almost all other practices, even other Zen schools, you are constantly told to practice in order to get somewhere. People who practice this way are using their zazen in order to get something more. They've got different degrees and ranks and techniques to obtain what they want, or what they think they want. They even use their breathing to get ahead in their practice. Almost all masters today teach you to count breaths. They've developed a system where you count your breaths up to ten and back down to one. That's just a gimmick. It doesn't help you to understand that the Way does not depend on your practice or your awakening.

> **The Dharma vehicle is free and unhindered.**
> **What need can there be for the**
> **concentrated efforts of men?**

In his younger years, at a Tendai temple on Mount Hiei, Dogen asked this very question. Though he was already a disciple of Master Koin, he was still a simple practitioner. He had doubts. His thinking had yet to mature. He still thought with the ordinary mind of a *sotapanna*, a person just starting out in the practice of the Way.

One day, he asked Master Koin, "Since it is written in the sutras that all human beings have Buddha nature, why do we have to do all this hard zazen? Since we all have Buddha nature, why do we need to realize it? Why do we need to have satori?"

Master Koin didn't respond. Perhaps he said nothing to Dogen because there was nothing to say. At any rate the young Dogen was disappointed by his silence.

Some time later, Master Koin said to him, "Look, Dogen, you should go see the Rinzai master Eisai Zenji. He knows better than I do." Eisai actually was a Zenji. Rinzai people like titles and ranks. In our Soto tradition, the heads of Eihei-ji and

Soji-ji temples are called Zenji, but in general other masters can only become Zenji after their death.

So Dogen went off to find Eisai. It was an arduous trip for someone who only wanted to ask a question. He found Eisai and asked him, "Why practice, since we all have Buddha nature right from the start?"

Eisai answered, "Not one of the many buddhas in the three worlds knows he's a Buddha. But cats and oxen do know."

The three worlds are the past, the present, and the future. They could also be the visible world, the invisible world, and the beyond. Obviously, it's only a manner of speaking, because we can obtain satori in none of these incarnate worlds – incarnate because they are subject to *samsara*, the cycle of transmigration. No buddha, not one of the many buddhas, "knows he's a buddha. But cats and oxen do know." This is not a *koan*, but a figurative way of speaking. It means that no buddha, no awakened person, thinks that he has or does not have Buddha nature. The awakened person never says to himself, "I've got satori and that guy over there doesn't." That sort of thing is unawakened, ordinary thinking. "But cats and oxen do know": only an animal, only the mind of illusion, thinks that way.

The first time I came across this way of looking at things – particularly when I first heard this story – I was very struck by it because it meant that people who do zazen are no better than those who do not. I mean "better" in the sense that those who do zazen will get something that others won't. You almost always hear the opposite: "Hey! If you don't do zazen, tough luck for you!"

But that doesn't mean that we should level things out, use the mountains to fill in the valleys and make everything flat. Sensei used to tell us sometimes, in a different context, that if you give a *fuse*, a gift of money, to a real Zen monk, then the merit is vast, while if you give the same money to a beggar, the merit is negligible. I think that's true too, and that's why I was struck by the story of Dogen and Eisai.

In truth, the Great Body is well beyond the dust of the world. Who could think it possible to clean it?

Master Dogen is alluding here to the well-known story of two of Master Konin's disciples, Jinshu and Eno. Konin, the fifth patriarch, asked his disciples to write a poem demonstrating their understanding and wisdom.

Jinshu wrote:

The body is the Bodhi tree.
The mind is a bright mirror.
Constantly, we clean and polish it,
So that no dust may obscure it.

Eno, in response to Jinshu, wrote:

There is no Bodhi tree,
And no shining mirror.
In the end all is empty,
Where then could dust alight?

Jinshu's poem compares Buddhist practice – zazen, *gyoji* – to cleaning a mirror, while Eno is saying that originally there is no impurity and thus no need to clean anything at all. These two positions had already been around for a long time, since before Bodhidharma came to China. They still exist today, although the difference is less clear-cut. Now most people discredit Jinshu's ideas – called the Gradual School – and claim to be part of Eno's school of thought – called the Sudden Enlightenment School. The Soto lineage descends directly from Eno, while Jinshu's line disappeared shortly after his death.

Eno's poem illustrates the idea that truth and illusion cannot be separated from each other. This idea is fundamental. In order to grasp Zen teaching, it is absolutely essential to understand this in your body, and not just in your head. It's a question of mind. Eno is talking about a complete 180-degree turn in our minds, while Jinshu sees gradual progress, day by day, little by little. Jinshu was Konin's number-one disciple and he knew absolutely everything – how to do the ceremonies and what was written in the sutras, for example – but he could never have been a true master. Eno was a true master, and Konin recognized that by giving him his kesa and his bowl.

There is a Zen story in which a master tells his disciple to climb up a pole. When the disciple gets to the top, the master tells him to keep climbing. Jinshu climbed up a pole and got to the top; Eno climbed up a pole and kept on climbing, which is just another way of saying that he didn't climb anything at all. That's our teaching.

But I have to say that I have a soft spot for Jinshu, for two reasons. First, he taught the need to practice zazen daily, morning and evening. Come to the dojo, practice zazen, and, to quote Master Joshu, "if you haven't found the Way after ten years of practice, then you can cut off my head and use my skull as a wash basin."

Second, I was impressed when I found out that it was because of Jinshu that Chinese people no longer had to bow down before their parents. Before that, if you wanted to talk to your mother and father, you had to get down on the ground in front of them. That was the tradition. But Jinshu gave a deeper meaning to *sampai*, or bowing. It is a gesture of respect for the Buddha, for the heart of every man, woman, child, and animal. Jinshu was banished from the capital because of this.

In the end, if you separate things, if you distinguish between truth and illusion, you express only one human point of view, created by your rational brain. Of course, everyone has his or her own point of view – even animals. For example, an owl thinks of the night as a human being thinks of the day. But those are only points of view. In Zen, no point of view concerns us. We are concerned with what is beyond that.

Master Sosan wrote, "Don't look for the truth. Content yourself with stopping *ken*." *Ken* means opinion or judgment, and it comes from our individual ego, our little self, which separates illusion and reality. We all have opinions, preferences, likes or dislikes, but it is important to realize that they are only personal. That way we can understand that there is no mirror to polish. We can understand *ku*.

> **It is never separate from anyone;
> it is always exactly where you are.
> Why go here or there to practice?**

"It" here means the Great Body, or if you prefer, the Way, Buddha nature.

The Way is right where you are. Why go off looking for it somewhere else?

We always want to go off somewhere. We want to take a vacation, and if we can't do that, then we want to move, change apartments, find something better. Or else we want to stay put, have our little comforts, not go climbing mountains. Some people see themselves as bad and they want to become good. Others see themselves as too good and would like to be seen as bad. It's hard to get beyond that.

During zazen you occupy a space that measures no more than a few square feet, and yet, if your practice is exact, if you do not hide in your personal thoughts, those few square feet contain the entire universe. So where is there to go? Where is there to stay?

Many people, before their encounter with the practice, with a master, with the Way, think it necessary to go off searching in faraway places. Some go off to Mexico on the trail of Don Juan, the Mexican Indian sage. Others leave for India or Japan. Master Deshimaru used to say, "You want to go to Japan? Okay, fine. Go as a tourist or go on business, but don't waste your time going for the Way. You want to visit temples? Go ahead. Take your camera, go in, spend ten or fifteen minutes, and leave."

There is a Taoist saying: "The great wise man lives in the street; the little wise man lives in the mountains."

So don't venerate a temple. It's just buildings that could easily be occupied by other people. Venerate what is highest, what makes you practice right where you are. Don't venerate the dojo, or the statue of Buddha, or the photo of the master on the altar. Venerate what is beyond all personal concepts.

This idea is present in many sutras. The *Lotus Sutra* says that the truth is very close, and that it is not complicated, but we cannot see it. We think the truth is something we have to travel far to find. We also think we have to define the truth, define satori. But defining it is missing the mark. We want to escape from where we are, avoid being here, living now. Or else we want to go back, go home, start over. But that's not possible either, so we feel regret, we feel loss, because we think that things were better before.

I have often heard older practitioners in the Deshimaru sangha say that things were better when the master was alive. Those who didn't know Master Deshimaru think that it was better when his close disciple Etienne Zeisler was still alive. I've heard people say that the old dojo on the rue Keller in Paris was better than the dojo we have now on the rue Tolbiac[1]. That's the truth slipping away from us, like the sky from the earth. That's *niho*: *ni*, "two" and *ho*, "dharma" or "existence." Two separate elements.

> **However, if there is a separation,**
> **be it ever so small, the Way is as distant**
> **as the sky from the earth.**

In 6th-century China, Sosan wrote the *Shinjinmei*, in which we find this verse:

> If a distinction as minute as a particle
> is created in the mind,
> An infinite distance immediately
> separates sky and earth.

Six centuries later, Dogen is saying the same thing in the *Fukanzazengi*. All the masters of the transmission, without exception, knew the *Shinjinmei*, and I imagine Dogen knew it by heart. All the basic Zen texts, with their different commentaries, have been passed down to us through the centuries. They were often transmitted orally. Master Deshimaru spent the last fifteen years of his life transmitting these texts, and his notes and commentaries on them, without adding or subtracting anything. It is the work of each master to pass on the tradition without adding any imaginative notions that his or her frontal brain might come up with. This work comes spontaneously and naturally from the instinctive brain.

And so we learn that if so much as a hair's breadth of separation appears between you and the Way, then your ego no longer coincides with your true nature; you yourself are no longer Buddha. If even the smallest difference exists at the outset, if authentic *shoshin* – beginning mind – does not appear, then later on you and Buddha will be a thousand miles apart. You create confusion in your mind: you create a subject which creates its object.

The relationship between Buddha and yourself is non-dualistic: not two, but one. Not even one, in fact. First the duality of Buddha vs. our little self disappears, then even that disappears. No more subject, no more object. This is true faith.

However, despite what you might hear in the Christian religion or even in some Buddhist circles, this doesn't mean that you have to get rid of your ego. A certain Zen master in the United States says repeatedly in his writing that the goal of our practice is to reduce the size of our ego until it finally disappears. This is completely childish! But if you want to think along those lines, then it's better if the ego were to get bigger and bigger. Master Deshimaru used to say, "I've got a super giant ego! An ego as big as the cosmos!" In other words, no more subject and object. It's the same as when the Buddha said, "When I had satori, all beings had satori." What you need is a vast mind. You shouldn't put it in a straitjacket and make it small by beating it over the head with endless prohibitions.

In the teaching as I received it from my master, ordination implies no prohibition. I once told that to some French Tibetan Buddhists, and they were shocked. How could I possibly say such nonsense! But it's true, nothing is forbidden. A real religious ordination carries with it no rules or prohibitions, because it is nothing other than the transformation of your karma. Look within yourself and be neither for nor against. The mind is not divided. That's what is important.

Once I was leading zazen at a dojo in London. During the *mondo*, a woman asked if she could do zazen alone at home when she couldn't come to the dojo. I thought about Master Deshimaru and answered the way I thought he would – same words, different mouth. I said, "As you like." Later, a monk came up to tell me that my answer had surprised him. He had spent twenty-five years in Japan with his master, had received the *shiho*, had translated the *Shobogenzo*, and wore the green kesa that only top-drawer monks can wear. He was also a non-drinking, non-smoking vegetarian, like his master. He was put off by my seemingly nonchalant attitude towards the practice. "Master Dogen and all the masters of the transmission say that you should practice zazen at least one hour every day!" he told me. On the other hand, he thought we were too strict in the dojo. "You take everything much too seriously. Don't move! Hard *kyosaku*! During the ceremony I saw that those who wear the kesa put down their *zagu* so the kesa doesn't touch the ground ..." He's a real monk, very sincere. His practice simply doesn't emphasize the same things that mine does.

Our teaching concerns only here and now in the dojo. What you do in your private life, whether you do zazen or go out drinking, is not important. What is important is here and now. What you do at home really isn't anybody's business. You should decide for yourself. So, please, don't make mistakes in the dojo, in your practice, or there will be separation between heaven and earth, between Buddha and you.

If even the slightest like or dislike arises, the mind is lost in confusion.

The slightest like – the smallest thought of love or preference – *or dislike* – hatred, scorn, the smallest shiver of distaste – and the truth evaporates, disappears.

In daily life our karma arises and, along with it, our illusions. The mind becomes troubled and confused. In Japanese this idea is represented by *shishu shin*, which means "lost mind." The mind gets lost, but not the truth. So we might sum up this teaching by saying that you shouldn't lose your mind.

In his poem conveying his understanding of the practice, Master Konin's disciple Jinshu expressed a preference: a rejection of dust. But Eno's thinking was absolutely perfect: no preference, no rejection, nothing, *mu*. He said that there was no mirror to be kept clean, and from that moment on he never wavered from that position throughout his life as monk and master. His mind was perfectly exact from the start and, consequently, remained perfectly exact to the end.

Of course, the word "mind" can mean several things, but we can simplify by saying that there is the small mind and the real mind. The real mind, as those experienced in the practice know, is the mind that fixes on nothing, that does not chase after its desires or follow its personal interests. The real mind is the mind that has returned to its natural condition. Few people have a normal mind – maybe saints and wise men and, of course, nuns and monks who practice zazen regularly and exactly.

Instead of being for this or against that, look inside yourself. Something that seems quite small at first, a tiny gap, will grow wider and wider. You can see this at work in your daily life: one thing becomes two, and then three, and soon heaven and earth are far apart. That separation is your karma at work, along with your *bonnos*, the illusions which complicate your mind.

But we are not helpless prisoners of our karma. Karma has brought us to where we are, but in this present moment, we can change it. Zen practice really begins when we see to what point our small mind clings to desire and rejects what it dislikes. Even those who have practiced for many years must continue to observe their attachments, especially when it comes to the notion of satori.

People who teach Zen sometimes run into this sort of thing: "*Godo!* I've got satori!"
"Is that right? What are you going to do with your satori?"
"Uh... Nothing."
"No point in having it then."

Recognizing your own wisdom, your own Buddha nature, your own satori, simply means following in the footsteps of others who have gone before. Zen leaves no trace behind. It has no odor. If someone is "very Zen," then he isn't Zen at all. At the end of the day, Zen is zazen, a return to the highest of spiritual quests within each of us.

*Imagine a person who is proud of his
understanding, filled with illusions about his
own enlightenment, who has barely glimpsed the
wisdom that penetrates all things, who has
entered the Way and cleared his mind,
giving rise to the desire to touch heaven itself.
Such a person has begun a preliminary
and limited exploration of the outer regions,
but he is still not completely on the vital Way
of absolute emancipation.*

Dogen is talking about people who think only of themselves, who can only see things from their own point of view. We all know that sort of person; sometimes that person is us. And when we're like that, a great abyss separates us from the Way, from any real religious practice.

Dogen wrote *shu sho ichi nyo*, which means "Practice and realization are one and the same." It's still an important point, since, even today in Soto Zen, many schools practice samadhi in order to be enlightened. The Zen of Dogen, of Kodo Sawaki, of Taisen Deshimaru, teaches that the practice of zazen and satori are one and the same. This is the Zen of sudden, immediate awakening, without degrees or progress or steps or ladders. It is free and unhindered because it is the present moment. Practice itself is realization: sudden unity.

*Need I speak of the Buddha,
who possessed innate knowledge?
We can still feel today the effect of the
six years he spent sitting completely still
in the lotus posture. And through Bodhidharma
the seal of the transmission has come down to us
and has preserved the memory of his nine years
of meditation in front of a wall.*

In the original text, Dogen refers to Buddha as "the sage of Jetavana." This was the park in Sravasti, India, which was given to Shakyamuni for his teaching. He spent nineteen rainy seasons there, doing zazen with his disciples.

So the sage of Jetavana *possessed innate knowledge*. That means that Buddha was born already awakened. And yet, awakened or not, he spent six years sitting under the Bodhi tree. Some say he sat there for six days. The number of days or years is not very important. What is important is that, even awakened, he still sat in the lotus posture, perfectly still, his spine perfectly straight. And we still practice the same thing 2,500 years later. Our zazen begins and ends under the Bodhi tree. Whether Buddha was born awakened or not isn't important, either. What is important is that although his nature, his real nature, was already awakened, he still sat in zazen, not just for six days, or six years, but his whole life through.

I don't know if Buddha sat facing the Bodhi tree, or facing away from it; but Bodhidharma, as far as we know, really did sit facing the wall. And what he handed down, *the seal of the transmission*, is not a piece of paper, an official written document, as is the case with some *shihos* today. It is the transmission of the awakened mind, *bodaishin*.

If Bodhidharma had never lived, then Zen as we know it would not exist. There are many legends about him. They say he walked all over northern China and that he crossed the Yangtse River on a reed. They say he spent nine years sitting in zazen without moving. Of course people exaggerate. We do know that he lived to an old age, one hundred and ten years or so, and that he came to China in the late 5th-early 6th century (the dates are uncertain), when Buddhism was known exclusively through the sutras. He wanted to show people that the true Way is practiced with the body and not just intellectually. So he did zazen in a cave in northern China, Shaolin, for many years. He didn't have a dojo. His disciple Eka didn't have one either, nor did Eka's disciple Sosan.

We don't need dojos or temples or books or sutras in order to transmit the real essence of the Dharma. Bodhidharma came to China with nothing but his body, and with that body he did zazen. He wanted to communicate the essence of the Dharma in a way that is not found in the sutras. Master Deshimaru used to say that the sutras were like texts written in the sand by the sea. Buddhism, and particularly Zen, relies on nothing. It's not based on the right brain, or the left brain, or a sheet of paper.

Bodhidharma was a patient, courageous man, not an adventurer. He didn't leave home to see new places or have fun. It was the same for Deshimaru when he came to France. He told us he had never been to Notre Dame or to the museums. He wasn't a tourist. He just practiced the Way. In the beginning he lived in the back of a store and did zazen on a cement floor. He didn't know anyone and he had no letters of introduction. That's unthinkable now. All the other masters who have come to the West from Japan have been sent by an organization. Bodhidharma didn't know anyone in China when he arrived either. He just went to Mount Suzan and practiced. People called him "the Brahman who stares at the wall."

Zazen. Za means "sitting"; *zen* means "concentration," or "tranquility." It's not the superficial tranquility that you feel when you go home, close the door behind you, and watch TV. It's absolute tranquility. It was there before you were born, it will be there after your death, and it is here, now.

Bodhidharma's Zen is not *shuzen*: Zen by degrees or stages. Bodhidharma's Zen is the confrontation with your innermost self, with what you have in your guts. The first years are easy. Five years – piece of cake. Ten years is a little harder. After fifteen or twenty years it's not easy at all. In fact, you have to be more careful then, because the path becomes more and more perilous. It's like the salmon swimming upstream to spawn its eggs and die: the journey is increasingly difficult. There's less and less water, more and more rocks, and a host of bears waiting on the banks to try and catch it. Those bears are everywhere in the practice: desire for honors, positions, ease, money, holiness, superiority... And so, many salmon never make it all the way upstream. They lose the source and lose their lives. It's the same with the practice. This is the highest of spiritual quests, and if it's easy, then it's not authentic.

Bodhidharma's Zen is simply natural and unconscious harmony with cosmic life, with nature, animals and people. Bodhidharma's name was well chosen. It was his master, Hannyatara, who gave it to him. *Bodhi* is "awakened" and *dharma* is "cosmic order" or "cosmic truth." So his name means "Awakened to the Cosmic Truth." Our practice, which is Bodhidharma's, begins and ends with zazen, and that zazen is like an acupuncture point: always the same point, the point that opens onto the entire universe, satori, cosmic truth, the Dharma.

Since it was thus for the saints of old, how could people today dispense with navigating the Way?

Who are the *saints of old*? For Dogen they were, among others, the patriarchs Bodhidharma, Eno, Obaku, Hyakujo, and Rinzai. They're not at all like Christian saints. The word is the same, but the meaning is completely different. For example, in Buddhism we say we are all saints, since we all have Buddha's satori, here and now. Also, especially in Zen, we talk about our "saints" in a more irreverent way than Christians do. "Obaku was an ancient Buddha," says Dogen in the *Shobogenzo*, "beyond time, greatly superior to Hyakujo, and much more acute than Baso. Rinzai, in comparison, was but a minor figure."

Dogen is talking about the founders and pillars of our teaching. Usually, we don't like to hear someone talk about our *saints of old* in terms of judgment, comparison, or categories – especially since we are taught that we shouldn't make such distinctions. In many schools, this sort of passage isn't cited. That's unfortunate, because we can use any means to teach.

Master Deshimaru was always comparing his disciples. "You're number one!" he would say, raising his thumb. Sometimes he turned thumbs down. "Foolish! You were number one, but now you're not even on the list!"

People from outside the sangha were shocked by his behavior and his teaching style. He had our Zen newsletter print a list that ranked his disciples. The list changed all the time, and you could watch your name move up or down. We all pretended it didn't matter. We tried to act as if we didn't care, as if we were beyond these kindergarten games. But we weren't at all; in fact, we took it very seriously. We had trouble sleeping at night when we went down on the list, and we slept like babies if we went up. We even got angry with each other over it.

This was Deshimaru's way of playing on people's ignorance. We all tend to compare ourselves with others and make categories. The master's work is to teach us detachment from the things that seem so important to our egos.

And so, according to Dogen, Obaku was superior to Hyakujo, more acute than Baso, and greater than Rinzai. Obaku lived at a time when Buddhism was persecuted by the Emperor – although Zen wasn't particularly targeted by the authorities, since the monks didn't own much of anything except for the huts where they did zazen. Here's an interesting story about the "saint of saints."

Prince Senso, the heir to the throne, practiced with Obaku. One day in the dojo, when Obaku was doing *sampai* towards the Buddha statue, Senso asked him, "Why do you bow before the Triple Treasure? What good are rituals when one is detached from any notion of awakening?"

Obaku slapped him.

Senso, his face turning purple, cried out in indignation, "Is that how a holy being shows himself?"

Obaku slapped him again.

"Really!" said Senso, "you are a vulgar man!"

Obaku slapped him a third time and said, "How about that one? Is it vulgar or refined?"

Obaku was twice the size of a normal man, so his hand covered Senso's face with every slap. Anyway, thanks to the strength of the last blow, it is said that Senso had satori.

At this time, Obaku was not a master, but a simple disciple. He was the *shusso*, or head monk, in Hyakujo's dojo, and Senso was his co-disciple. Given Senso's position as the emperor's son, slapping him around was certainly not a good way to get in good graces with the hierarchy – which shows that Obaku was no ordinary monk, and no ordinary saint.

Dogen is saying that the Buddhist saints threw themselves body and mind into the practice, so why shouldn't we? "We" in

13th-century Japan is no different than "we" in 21st-century Europe or America. When Dogen refers to "people today" not neglecting the practice, he is talking about himself and his disciples and the disciples of his disciples down to Kodo Sawaki and Taisen Deshimaru. He is telling us that, as much as possible, we all need to return to the great spiritual quest that is within us, and take people like Shakyamuni Buddha and Bodhidharma as examples.

In our practice we are proud that Shakyamuni Buddha was a real, historical person and not a mythical figure. He found satori on his own. He didn't ask God to help him. What was true for him is true for each of us. He said, "I have touched the mind. I have attained Buddhahood, and you are all future buddhas."

Kodo Sawaki, speaking of the *Fukanzazengi*, said, "Zazen is the exact, precise expression of the Dharma.... It expresses all aspects of the *Tathagata* [the buddha beyond all buddhas or, if you prefer, God]. Zazen itself realizes the Buddha's aspect and essence through the body of an individual human being. A new life depends on zazen."

Zazen is beyond Shakyamuni Buddha, beyond all buddhas, past, present, and future. In zazen, with our own individual body, we can make that real. We can create, as Kodo Sawaki says, a new life.

You must therefore abandon a practice based on intellectual understanding, running after words, and clinging to the letter.

Many people think that intellectual understanding is the deep truth; but it's really just words. And there's no reason to be limited by our understanding of a particular language. Grammar, conjugation, and spelling do not define us. If we weren't so attached to words, our world would be very different today. So don't base your practice on words, texts, or intellectual understanding.

One day someone asked the Buddha, "Why do ignorant people discriminate, while wise people do not?" The Buddha answered, "Because ignorant people cling to names, words, signs and labels."

It's a big problem in our society: the cause of wars. People chase after words and ideas. "I'm a Palestinian," or "I'm an Israeli." That's just ignorant thinking. We're not French or American or Palestinian or Israeli. We're not that small.

Many years ago, a *mondo* took place at the port of Mingchou between Dogen and an old *tenzo*, a temple cook, who had come there to buy mushrooms. Dogen was very young at the time but he was already a very learned monk. He had come to China to deepen his knowledge of Zen. He had looked everywhere, but found nothing that interested him. On the docks of Mingchou, he boarded a boat and was awaiting its departure for Japan, when he noticed an old monk who was drying some mushrooms in the sun. With curiosity, he watched the old man work in the heat of the day like a common laborer. He decided to speak to him, and discovered that the old monk was *tenzo* at Keitokuji temple. The two men talked, and their discussion has since become famous in Zen history.

"What are you doing out here in the hot sun?" asked Dogen.

"I must prepare these mushrooms for the temple. We're on sesshin."

"How far away is your temple?"

"A little over twenty miles from here."

"That's a long walk. I'd like to talk to you. Can you stay awhile?"

"No, I can't. I have to finish this work and get back."

The young Dogen – who wasn't so different from the scholarly young monks you might run into today – said, "But there must be many others in your temple who could replace you in the kitchen. You are old and you are obviously someone important."

"It is absolutely impossible to leave this work for someone else to do. Someone else is not me. Anyway, even if I wanted to stay, I would need the permission of the head of the temple, which I don't have."

Dogen wanted to keep the discussion going, so he pressed on:

"You must be at least sixty years old. Why are you doing this work? Why don't you devote your time to the study of sutras and other Buddhist texts?"

Which, of course, is what Dogen did all the time. Like a lot of people, he thought that reading books and sutras was more important than manual labor. Dogen had yet to learn about *samu* and *gyoji*. He had no idea that *mushotoku* even existed.

The *tenzo* looked him right in the eye and burst out laughing.

"My good monk, you don't know the true meaning of words. You know nothing of *bendo*. You have no idea how to practice the Way."

Upon hearing this reply, Dogen had a real shock. He broke out in a sweat – and it wasn't because of the sun. Later he would write in the *Tenzo Kyokun*, "A chill went through me and I was stunned for a long moment. I felt full of shame." One might think that Dogen had satori at that moment, but that's not at all what happened. When an authentic monk makes you realize that you've been mistaken, that you do not understand the true practice though you were convinced you did, then there's good reason to break out in a cold sweat. And so, Dogen was shaken up. Eventually he collected himself and continued the exchange.

"What is *bendo?*" he asked the *tenzo*. He might as well have asked, "What is the real world? What is the true Way?" *Bendo* means finding the Way through the practice.

The old man answered, "Practice your question and you will become a true disciple of the Way."

Dogen wanted to keep talking but the *tenzo* said, "I must return to the temple now. If you want to come, you will certainly be welcome there."

According to Master Deshimaru, after this encounter with the old cook, Dogen was truly transformed; he did a complete about-face, and everything changed for him. He had to turn his attention inward instead of outward as he had always done before. As we know, he did go to Nyojo's temple, Keitokuji, where he saw the *tenzo* again, and asked him, "What is the true meaning of words?" The *tenzo* replied, "One, two, three, four." Which means that the Way is present everywhere, and that it is not hidden.

The story of Dogen and the *tenzo*,[2] and the passage from the *Fukanzazengi* it illustrates, are not telling us that reading and study are bad. They're just telling us *how* to read and study. Read with the eye of the Way. The eye of the Way is not a natural gift. It is a gift of the tradition. That's what Dogen started to understand on that hot day at the port of Mingchou. Up until then he had been cerebral; for him, cooking and drying mushrooms were not the essence of Zen. The old monk who had walked so far to buy mushrooms and prepare them was simply beyond his comprehension.

More than seven centuries have gone by since this story took place, but things haven't changed much. We could even say that time doesn't really exist. Today, most people who come to the practice start out with the same sort of mind. I know I did. We think, like Dogen, that in order to be a monk all you really need to do is ask for the ordination. Of course, you also have to learn the posture, learn how to act in the dojo, learn the ceremonies, and maybe, if you have an intellectual bent, read a few of the important sutras. As if being a monk or a nun were some kind of position, like a job in a corporation. You get the title of "monk" or "nun" and then you go on with life pretty much as before, with the same mind, the same attitudes and habits. That's a very poor understanding of the teaching and the sutras. By the same token, if you do zazen with a goal in mind – even a very tiny, almost invisible goal – then your zazen is false. Becoming a monk in those circumstances only strengthens your false thinking.

When you receive the ordination, you don't become someone or something special. You become no one and nothing, in the deepest sense. For me, Bodhidharma's words are one of the best descriptions of what a Zen nun or monk really is: *kakunen musho* – "infinite sky, no holiness/no madness."

You must learn to turn and direct your light
inward to illuminate your true nature.
Body and mind will fall away, and your original face
will appear. If you want to reach thusness,
then you must practice thusness without delay.

Here is the same thing expressed another way: "After returning to the normal condition thanks to your posture in zazen, your body and mind spontaneously vanish, and automatically, naturally and unconsciously, your true self appears. If you want to attain that state, then you should practice zazen right away."

Master Deshimaru used to talk about turning inward, about the mind that turns completely around. After that there is no more mind, no more inside and outside. You will no longer be taken in by appearances, forms, or bodies. "My male body" or "my female body": that's false thinking, too. At birth our mind is neither male nor female. When you take away the frills and the decorations, reality appears.

A monk arrives at the temple and the master asks him, "Where do you come from?"

The monk could give all sorts of answers but generally he gives his address – the street, the town or village – and, if the master is easygoing, he'll say, "Okay. You don't understand, but that's all right. You can come in." But a more severe master might say, "Go away! You don't understand anything." What the master wants to know is whether or not you understand your true nature. How far is it from your street, your town or village, to your real nature?

When Dogen says that body and mind will fall away, he's talking about what happens during zazen. You return to the normal condition and your body/mind spontaneously drops away. At that moment you realize your true self. Here again, Dogen is referring to his own experience, his meeting with Master Nyojo.

Master Nyojo was not often angry, but sometimes, if a monk made a mistake in zazen, he could be furious. Most masters are not like that these days. They're always very nice. You can't really get angry, because people don't like it and they leave. Anyway, one day a monk sitting in zazen next to Dogen fell asleep. Nyojo got up and, according to Master Deshimaru, hit him violently over the head with his sandal. Then he threw him off the platform.

Nyojo shouted, "*Shin jin datsu raku!*" Then he announced, "That's it! No more zazen today! No more teaching! The sesshin is over!" and he stalked off to his room.

Young Dogen followed him there, did *sampai* before him, and repeated the words that the master had said, "*Shin jin datsu raku.*" He went on, "Today I had a great shock. My body and mind have completely changed, have completely turned around."

Nyojo wasn't angry any more. He answered, "*Datsu raku shin jin.*"

He meant, "Keep going. Keep on ridding yourself of mind and body until the end of your life." Nyojo really was a very great master.

Later, in the *Shobogenzo*, Dogen was to define *shin jin datsu raku*. He says that when a being becomes a buddha, he is not changed. His body and mind have simply dropped away.

Kodo Sawaki said that *shin jin datsu raku* is "to abandon selfishness, to believe in the Buddha and follow him." Okubo, a 20th-century expert on Buddhism, said that it means "to forget your attachment to yourself and become one with the Dharma." But I particularly like my own master's explanation: "*Shin jin* is body and mind, and *datsu raku* is bad karma transformed." That differs greatly from what you often hear in many Zen schools today, where *datsu raku* is interpreted as satori, or awakening. So, more and more often, *datsu raku* becomes Dogen's satori. Big mistake.

If you want to understand Master Dogen you have to understand *shin jin datsu raku*, and you also have to understand Nyojo's answer, *datsu raku shin jin*, which means, "don't stop there, keep going." There is no satori. That way, satori never stops.

Books and magazines and TV and cinema all insist that our practice must have a goal: attaining *kensho* or satori, for example. Otherwise, the media can't make sense of what we do, and they have nothing to say about Zen. So they add their own simplistic ideas. What's important is not what the media think, but the way each of us walks on the Way, the way each of us practices thusness, or *inmo*, or "what is."

Lee Lozowick, a master in the Baul tradition, once came to visit the Paris Dojo and La Gendronnière Temple. He gave a lecture during which he said that the problem with Zen is that the teaching stays in the dojo and doesn't seep into our daily lives. That may be the case for some people. It's true, for example, that as monks and nuns, we don't wear our robes out in the street, in daily life, and perhaps some people need that constant support or reminder. But you have to live in the invisible world, which is everywhere. Invisible as in no separation. In the dojo or outside of it, our practice is the same. The question is how to be in the present moment, for everyone's benefit. Not in an altruistic sense, but in the sense that there is no separation between ourselves and others. Our teaching is all about how to live in this world. You have to understand that Zen is at work in everyday life. Otherwise, this practice would have no meaning: the life of Shakyamuni Buddha would be meaningless, as would the lives of Tibetan saints such as Milarepa. They, and all the others, greatly helped our human world.

So if you want to reach "what is," then you must practice "what is" right now. The dojo is one place to do this. You're sitting facing a wall. You're not chasing after your thoughts, or trying to avoid them. Consciously or unconsciously, you follow your breathing – long and deep – without wanting anything at all. That's our practice in the dojo and in everyday life as well: being awakened along with all other beings, with the entire earth.

Chapter Two
Zazen Posture

Everything I have talked about so far – the first page of this three-page text – is only an introduction. What follows is the core of this "Universal Guide to the Practice of Zazen": a detailed description of the basic practice as Dogen learned it from his master, Nyojo, and as it is still taught in the Soto School today.

Dogen talks about the place where you do zazen, describes the correct mental attitude for sitting, and explains the posture in detail: the position of the legs, hands, back, head, mouth, eyes, and nose. It's interesting to note that when he describes the posture, Dogen's terminology is exactly like ours. Practicing the Way of real Zen is no different now than it was in the 13th century.

And so, as Master Deshimaru said, "Here is where this powerful text really begins: how to enter into zazen."

For sanzen, a quiet room is best.

Sanzen is an interesting word. Master Deshimaru used this word in his first translation of the *Fukanzazengi*. But since he wrote elsewhere that sanzen was like zazen, in the new translations we use the word zazen. But *sanzen* is more than just zazen. It's the same *zen* – meditation or tranquility – but with the addition of *san*, meaning "to unite or bring together."

When Dogen was still a disciple, he asked his master one day, "What is zazen?"

"Zazen is *sanzen*," answered Nyojo. "Practice with a master. Master and disciple."

What does it mean to practice with a master? What is a master? What is a disciple? Practitioners in many Western countries have stopped using the words "master" and "disciple." They say "teacher" and "student" instead. I suppose they want to do away with any notion of power and submission. But I think those words aren't strong enough. It's as if class is over when you leave the dojo.

You can define "master" any way you want, but for a disciple it's the person who can show you the Way. Not only through his teaching in the dojo, but also through his behavior in the world, through what he really is beyond his personality or the disciple's personality. The master is the one who shows you the practice by practicing with you: *san*, "together." He's the one who can transmit his own master's teaching, while the disciple is the one who is open to that teaching and that practice. The disciple obliges the master to practice, and vice-versa. In the end, master and disciple are interchangeable. They are together in the heart of the practice and in the spirit of *i shin den shin*, my mind to your mind. The master is not necessarily alive. My master is dead now, but I will always be his disciple. It is a relationship of mutual service, not for ourselves but for the Dharma. The work of a monk or nun, a true disciple, is to pass that on.

If you do not have such a relationship, the practice becomes harder and harder. It gets harder for the disciple too, but for the person who has no master it becomes unbearable in the end. This is not something I read in a book; it's what I have seen in my life, what I have seen and still see around me. There are people who don't have that sort of relationship and who would like to have it. That's already a false state of mind. Nobody is going to help you find anything. I often hear questions like, "Do you think I should look for a master?" I don't think it's a question of looking – unless you're looking inside yourself. Because, in the end, the real master is you, your real self, your real nature. But in order to find that inner master, an external master is necessary.

A quiet place is best. Sensei often said that the dojo on rue Pernety was a good place. "For Paris," he said, "this is really a quiet dojo." Our temple, La Gendronniére, is usually a quiet place too, although sometimes we have had to work hard at keeping the peace. During one summer camp I directed there, a distant but pervasive noise like that of a broken washing machine began filling the dojo during the morning zazen. As we usually do in such cases, I sent my *shusso* out to see what the disturbance was. I expected him to come back in a few minutes with an explanation, but when the end of zazen arrived there was no sign of him. Finally, several hours later, he returned in his car. He was still wearing his kolomo and kesa and clutching a *kyosaku*. Apparently the noise was coming from a rave party somewhere in the vicinity, and he had spent his time trying to track it down, without success; the noise went on through the night. It's true, a quiet place is best – but good luck finding one.

Several of my co-disciples and I continue to teach and practice in Paris in a large dojo on the rue Tolbiac, which we acquired in 1996. It is a protected historical building consisting of 770 square meters on three levels around a courtyard. The dojo itself measures 120 square meters. It's bigger and quieter than our previous dojos, and funded entirely by the membership fees and generosity of those who practice with us, since we don't have a system of tax-deductible donations like the Americans have.

We might imagine that conditions were somewhat more primitive for the "saints of old." Here is what Master Keizan advised his disciples in the late 13th century:

"When you sit in zazen, don't prop yourself up against a wall or a door or any such thing. Do not sit where the wind is blowing. Do not sit in high open places. Do not sit where there are fires. Do not sit where there are floods or bandits. Do not sit facing the sea. [He's right about that: it's not a good idea to face the horizon. You're better off facing a wall.] Do not sit where it is too bright or too dark, too hot or too cold. Do not sit with hoodlums, noisy people or loose women."

Personally, I don't have a problem sitting with hoodlums and loose women, as long as they sit still and don't break the silence.

Naturally, when you've gotten into the habit of doing zazen, you can practice anywhere at any time. You don't need a dojo. You don't need a Buddha statue or even a zafu. I've practiced sitting on my shoes, on telephone books, and on rolled-up blankets. An experienced practitioner can practice at a busy intersection in a noisy city, or completely alone. Either way, it is as if you are on a mountain. *Mushin* – no mind – is the real mountain. That's what Master Dogen is saying, from the very first paragraph of the *Fukanzazengi*. The Way is where you are. Why go elsewhere? The real dojo is under the sky. Just be careful where you step, whether it be in a dojo, a temple, a room, or a cave.

Eat and drink moderately.

When you do zazen you should only eat about two-thirds of what you usually eat. During a sesshin you figure that out pretty quickly, because if you eat too much, your joints hurt and you feel sleepy. Everyone knows it, but not everyone practices it.

Almost all American and Japanese dojos practice *oryoki*, the mealtime ceremony using several bowls. The literal meaning of *oryoki* is "just enough": don't take more than you need. Don't keep a reserve of food, either. It's the same with zazen. Don't hold back energy in zazen. Give it all, here and now.

Though some of Master Deshimaru's disciples have adopted this complex way of eating, most of us follow a simpler version, adapted to the food we eat in the West: one bowl, one spoon. In Deshimaru's time we didn't use bowls at all. We ate on plates, with forks and knives, like everyone else. Perhaps if he had lived longer we would have started doing *oryoki*. One could say that he died at the right time, because this way, our practice has remained European. In Japanese Zen they tell you how to do everything – not only how to eat but also how to go to the toilet, how to bathe, how to sleep. The point is to be aware of what you're doing. If they're done in the spirit of the Way, then eating, sleeping, bathing, and going to the toilet become as important as breathing.

Put aside all engagements
and abandon all business.

Of course, you don't abandon your business when you're supposed to be taking care of business. But during zazen you set aside the business of your daily life. That's one of the reasons why we wear black kimonos or kolomos in the dojo, and take off our makeup, jewelry, socks, and watches. It's good to put aside the things that tie us to the ordinary world.

During zazen, no positions are taken. You don't think about things being good or bad. You just observe your thoughts and concentrate on your posture and your breathing.

The *Gion Shogi*, a text by Fuyodokai, a master who lived in the 11th century, contains this startling sentence: "Monks should hate the foul work of the mind, be above life and death, and reject complicated relationships." For a long time I didn't really understand that way of looking at things. I thought that when Fuyodokai said, "reject complicated relationships," he meant reject complicated, pain-in-the-neck people. I finally understood that what he meant is that I should reject my own mental activity.

Don't think, "This is good" or "That is bad."

Thinking that something is good or bad is taking a position, a moralistic point of view. It's not free-flowing thought. You can even say that it's not the normal condition. The Eightfold Path that Shakyamuni Buddha taught after his awakening tells us that we should have right understanding, right thinking, right concentration, etc. But just what is right understanding? Or right thinking? It is, for example, when you look at something or someone without thinking of anything or anyone else. But if you have ideas like "that's good" or "that's bad," then you can't see clearly because you're only looking at things from one moralistic or personal point of view. That's not right understanding. That's just subjective thinking.

So look only once. Don't look twice. That's how the awakened mind works, because for the awakened mind, the present moment is complete. Obviously there's no judgment, no petty personal ideas, no analysis. Look once. That's eternity in a single instant.

I remember hearing Master Deshimaru saying to someone, "You shouldn't sit on a moralistic zafu." But not being moralistic doesn't mean that you're against good morals. An awakened person, no matter what she desires, always remains, automatically and unconsciously, within the realm of morality; whereas an ordinary person, though she may preach morality, easily falls into error. Being able to immediately distinguish between true and false, between good and bad, is fundamental. That's Buddha mind. But if you try to follow other people's morality, if you force yourself into a mold, then you're not free and you will make mistakes.

In Confucius's time there was a famous thief named Toseki who could steal anything from anyone. Toseki had a hideout in the mountains. Confucius greatly desired to meet him because he thought he could educate and reform him. As you know, Confucius's ideas about education were mostly based on morality, on what's right and what's wrong. Anyway, Confucius sent out the word that he would be happy to meet the thief and, one day, Toseki sent his men to find Confucius. "Okay, if you want to see Toseki, come with us. We'll guide you." The trip took a long time because the thieves had to be sure that the authorities weren't following them. Finally Confucius arrived and was presented to Toseki. He immediately tried to educate the thief. All that Confucius really knew how to do was educate people. But very quickly Toseki interrupted him. "Stop! You're nothing but a childish little man. You only see one side of things. You can preach to others if you want, but not to me. Goodbye and don't come back." It was a big setback for Confucius – but not for the truth.

One day in Paris, I came upon two men trying to steal my motorbike, an old Solex on its last legs. They had arrived on a beautiful new bike, but they wanted mine, too. But I caught them in the act, and they got the worst of it. In the end I found myself with two bikes. The next day, after *genmai*, I told the story to Master Deshimaru. He really liked it – he made me repeat it at least ten times. Afterwards I said, "But Sensei, I did steal, after all..."

"You know what stealing is?" he asked.

"No, what?"

"Just objects changing places."

If Master Deshimaru had gone to visit Toseki the thief, maybe he would have profoundly changed his mind – something Confucius could not accomplish with his morality. It's true, "Do not steal" is one of the ten *kai*, or Buddhist precepts; but it's not a moralistic law, it's a universal law.

In Buddhism, and more particularly in Zen, we go beyond good and evil. It's hard to understand evil. But then, it's hard to understand goodness, too.

That makes me think of the fifth verse of the *Shinjinmei*:

The struggle between right and wrong in our conscience
Leads to a sick mind.

It makes you mentally ill. That's one of the big problems in our civilization. Suffering is no longer mostly physical, but mental. I'm not just talking about people in psychiatric wards, but about everybody. Almost everyone thinks exclusively with the frontal brain and completely forgets the instinctive, primitive brain.

But when you do zazen, you learn to let the frontal brain rest while you think with the hypothalamus, with the body and with the *hara*. You learn through the posture while breathing from the body's center of gravity in the abdomen. Little by little you come back to what Master Deshimaru called the normal condition. "The complete expression of a human being," he said, "comes from the reduction and elimination of the subconscious" – in other words, the elimination of the superficial. The subconscious has to come up and come out, and then you become clear and simple, and your karma is set aside. The real practice of zazen starts once you have returned to the normal condition. For some it takes a long time, while others get there quickly. But even if it comes quickly, that doesn't necessarily mean that your practice will deepen. Most people practice for years, understand the teaching, have a little satori, and then stay there, not going any further. But when you stop, you start to slide back. If you start to practice you shouldn't stop, because it is said that a person who enters the Way and then leaves it will never find it again in this life.

When, in the normal condition, you find your originality, you also discover your real individuality, your real personality. A lot of people think that you lose it. Absolutely not. You find it and you blossom out. Of course, you shouldn't confuse a big ego with real individuality. One has nothing to do with the other.

What is the normal condition? We could say *shiki soku ze ku, ku soku ze shiki*: form is emptiness, emptiness is form. Don't cling to emptiness, and don't cling to form. That's the normal condition, the highest truth. If you do that, then you will be in the present moment, present in reality. What could be truer than that? It has to flow like a river. Wisdom can only work in that flow.

When we have no worries in life, we live like *devas*. We've got it all. At those times, *shiki* being *ku* and *ku* being *shiki* is not hard to practice. But when we have problems, when our minds are a little sick from contradictions and judgments, then it gets harder. That's why it's especially important to do zazen when things aren't going well, because it gives you a chance to observe yourself objectively and to really understand yourself and others. We shouldn't avoid difficulty, but rather use every occasion as a chance to practice the Way and to really, deeply liberate ourselves. That's why Master Unmon said, "Every day is a good day." In my experience, monks and nuns are not unhappy people. I have had some serious difficulties in my life, and I suffer like everyone else. But today, this suffering no longer makes me unhappy. On the contrary, I find it very interesting. It provides me with an opportunity and an instrument, a way of observing what's happening. Now when things are going badly, I practically rub my hands together and roll up my sleeves – and it's not masochism! When things are going well, I'm very careful. But when things are bad, first of all I do my best not to show it, and then it really intrigues me, and gets me to look at myself. It's as if I'm drawn to my zafu. Before I began Zen practice, my suffering was more muted, but it sometimes lasted for years. Today I notice that though the pain is particularly acute, it passes much more quickly, thanks to the practice.

Do not take sides for or against.
Stop all movement of the conscious mind.

Neither for nor against. That might seem easy, but I think it's actually quite hard. We're constantly taking sides, and when we take one side we reject the other. All day long we take sides – usually the side that seems most favorable to our personal interests at any given time. We're always defending ourselves. All you have to do is listen to yourself and you'll observe not only that you're defending yourself – "It's not fair!" "I'm right and she's wrong!" – but also how confused your mind is at the same time.

Observing yourself that way is the practice of zazen outside the dojo. It's easier not to take sides when you're sitting in zazen. But as soon as you go outside you start excluding something or someone and including yourself. If you look at yourself honestly it's enough to drive you to despair. You say to yourself, "I've been doing zazen for fifteen or twenty years and I'm still confused. I'm still hung up on right and wrong, good and bad." A lot of people start to think that maybe zazen doesn't work. And they're right. It doesn't.

We say, "Don't follow your thoughts." But who can stop them once they start to line up in your head? I don't think anyone can – unless you practice some sort of ascetic mortification with all sorts of prohibitions. But the Zen that I was taught and that I teach does not prohibit anything. So you might wonder, in the end, "What good does it do to practice, since it doesn't work?"

At that point, you should remember the story of Jinshu, Eno, and the mirror. Jinshu said we must keep polishing the mirror. Eno said there is no mirror, there is nothing to polish. Master Deshimaru once asked, "Why didn't Jinshu receive the transmission? My disciples have to understand ..." I don't think that this practice can take us anywhere if we think that it's supposed to work or that it's supposed to lead us somewhere step by step, which is Jinshu's idea. Rather, we should try to understand Eno's position, that everything is now, and that even the idea of progress in Zen is an act of taking sides. It's hard to understand and harder to explain. Of course, thinking that there's no mirror and no dust is also a judgment, a position. But...

Nensokan: nen is "consciousness," *so* means "thinking," and *kan* means "observation." *Nensokan* is "awareness of the moment." But if we try to hold on to that awareness, we're giving in to a desire to progress, and then this awareness of the present moment becomes thoughts and pictures. If we can simply stop holding on, naturally of course, then we can become strong and hopeful. Sensei always said, "Strong! You must be strong!" He talked like that but he wasn't macho. He meant strong like nature, like trees and flowers and butterflies. Strong, for him, didn't mean becoming strong in karma but rather having a strong trust and unshakable faith in the cosmic system.

How do you stop the movement of the conscious mind? By not taking sides for or against, by not discriminating between true and false. Dogen says "stop"; but I don't think you can really stop the movement of consciousness. You can observe it. You can slow it down or transform it. But in order to do that you have to not choose. That's one of the major themes in all the old Zen texts.

It is well put in these lines from the *Sanshodoei*:

Unsullied, the moonlight dwells in the waters of the mind.
Even the waves break upon it and become light.

The conscious mind is the personal mind. So, *stop all movement of the conscious mind* means don't be guided by your personal consciousness. That's possible in zazen. But in order for it to happen, you shouldn't even want it, because that, too, is personal thinking. During zazen, be like a shadow on a mirror, which passes and leaves no trace.

**Do not judge your thoughts or viewpoints.
Do not desire to become a buddha.**

You have to stop all intellectual considerations, even those expressed through thoughts or mental images of the Buddha or, if you prefer, images of purity, or God. This idea is well illustrated in a *mondo* between Master Nangaku and his disciple Baso:

Nangaku happened upon Baso doing zazen.

"You are doing zazen, but are you doing it with a goal in mind?" asked the master.

"I'm doing zazen to become a buddha," replied the disciple.

Nangaku picked up a tile and began to polish it.

"What are you doing, master?" asked Baso.

"I'm polishing a tile in order to make it a mirror."

"But, it can't be done!"

Don't waste your time trying to become a buddha or to become pure. Don't try to become anything. Or, as Sosan puts it in the Shinjinmei, "Do not seek the truth."

**Zazen has absolutely nothing
to do with sitting or lying down.**

You have to understand this with your body. A master should understand that you don't explain the Dharma with your mouth; a disciple should understand that you don't practice zazen with your legs. Zazen isn't limited to the seated posture. It's not just a matter of crossing your legs, keeping your back straight and your chin in. Remember the beginning of the *Fukanzazengi* where Dogen clearly states that zazen itself is Buddha: no separation.

I am sometimes asked if it's possible to do zazen lying down. If that's the best you can do – in other words, if you are bedridden or paralyzed or otherwise incapacitated, and not just hanging around in bed hoping to sleep a little longer – then yes, you can practice zazen lying down. The breathing will be slightly different than in the seated posture, but otherwise it's the same: don't follow your thoughts.

*At the place where you usually sit, spread out
a thick mat and place a cushion upon it.
Sit either in the lotus or the half-lotus posture.
In the lotus posture, first place your right foot
on your left thigh, and then your left foot
on your right thigh. For the half-lotus,
simply place the left foot on the right thigh.*

Dogen wrote this text six months after his return to Japan. Until then, few people in that country knew about the posture. It was the same when Master Deshimaru came to France in 1967. Nobody knew about zazen. But today, thanks to the practice in the dojos, and also thanks to the media – articles in the press, radio and television programs – even people who have never practiced know about the lotus position.

This posture existed long before Shakyamuni Buddha. He didn't invent it. There are texts that are thousands of years old that refer to the lotus position. They say "lotus" or "triangle of fire" or "the burning triangle." The lotus is not only associated with sovereignty, with the notion of highness and majesty – the most majestic of human postures – but also with the crossed legs of the Buddha and of all the buddhas before Shakyamuni. The lotus flower is a powerful symbol. It grows in mud, but when it reaches the water's surface it blossoms and flowers with incomparable purity and perfection. In Zen dojos and temples, after meals or *mondos*, the master recites the *Shi shi kai*, which means, "In this world of ku (emptiness) may we live in muddy water with the purity of the lotus."

When I refer to the lotus posture I really don't make any distinction between the lotus and the half-lotus. In the lotus the feet stimulate important acupuncture points on the thighs that correspond to the liver, the kidneys, and the gallbladder. In the half-lotus the foot only stimulates one side at a time. But if you're sitting in the middle of your zafu and your knees are pressed firmly on the floor, then the balance is almost the same. The posture is complete in either the lotus or the half-lotus. Both postures combine the perfect position of the body with deep breathing. Sometimes people ask me, "Why the right foot first? Why not the left foot?" The answer is that there's no reason at all. It's just an example. Dogen could have explained it the other way around. You can start with the left foot if you want – either way, it's exactly the right posture.

Through the practice of this posture, along with deep breathing and a fluid mind that fixes on nothing, we can touch the heart, the center of perfect stability and tranquility that is in each of us and in the Buddha. We can align body and mind in *jakujo*, "absolute tranquility."

Be sure to loosen your belt and your clothing and arrange them properly. Next put your right hand on your left foot and your left hand on your right palm, with the palms turned upward and the tips of your thumbs touching. Sit up straight without leaning to the left or right, forward or backward. Make sure that your ears are lined up with your shoulders, and your nose with your navel. Put your tongue against the front of the palate. The mouth is closed and the teeth touch. Always keep your eyes open and breathe gently through your nose.

... loosen your belt and your clothing ... Notice that Dogen doesn't say anything here about kimonos, kolomos, or kesas. *Fukan* means "recommended to the people," to society, not just to monks and nuns. So he's talking about street clothes.

Zen is, above all, coming to the dojo and doing zazen with other people. It doesn't matter whether you're wearing pants or a skirt or a kolomo or a kesa. It doesn't matter whether you're a complete beginner or a master with the *shiho*. In zazen there is no difference. Zen is simplicity. A simple posture. That's why we can practice with such determination for so many years, for an entire lifetime.

... left hand in right hand ... The left hand represents *ku*: empti-ness, the spiritual; and the right hand represents *shiki*: things, the material world. We put the left hand over the right hand because we receive the spiritual, not only through the master but by sit-ting all together in dojo. Buddha, on the other hand, places the right hand in the left because he *gives* the spiritual. Same thing when we enter the dojo left foot first. It's because we are aware of entering the world of *ku*. When we leave the dojo right foot first, we are returning to the world of *shiki*, the material world.

The position of the hands influences the brain. The hands form the shape of an egg. The edges of the hands press against the lower abdomen. There is a slight tension in the thumbs as they touch each other, forming neither mountain nor valley. We can think of the left side as representing one thing and the right side representing another, but in the end the left is the right and the right is the left. When you put the two sides together, legs crossed and one hand on the other, you can't tell which is which, because zazen and satori are one and the same thing.

The waist stretches and the pelvis tips slightly forward from the first mobile vertebra at the base of the spinal column, just above the coccyx. This is the key point in the posture: find it, and you can correct your posture, create perfect balance, and breathe deeply. The abdominal muscles are open, neither tense nor completely relaxed. People who have done a lot of zazen have calm muscles and a calm body, which means they can think with their bodies.

... tongue against palate ... mouth closed ... teeth touching ... This might be difficult when you're starting out in the practice, but it gets easier. Twenty years ago I found that this position made my jaw stiff. But it doesn't now, because when you draw up the

nape of the neck and pull in your chin, then the teeth come together naturally.

An open mouth is not an awakened posture. Neither is having the mouth closed and the jaws open. The position of the tongue is also important. There are people who have been pressing the tip of their tongue up against their front teeth since their childhood. In some cases they have even deformed the line of their mouth. That's not right either. The tip of the tongue should just touch the front of the palate, and the mouth and the jaw should be closed naturally.

Such a corporal attitude is also a sign of determination. Determination should always be present in the posture, in the face, in the hands and the feet. Zazen isn't calisthenics or gymnastics. It's not a martial art or yoga or any other sort of meditation. It is more simply, or more deeply, our personal quest touching the very heart of our body and mind.

... *eyes open* ... Master Hettsu says that those who do zazen with their eyes closed are like the demons of the black cave. This "cave of demons" (or, sometimes, "the cave in the black mountain") is a Zen metaphor. Life inside the cave of demons is like the life of a person shut up alone with his ego. When you close your eyes you can feel at home with your fantasies, daydreams, and imagination. But that's not the deep peace of zazen. Zazen isn't the cave of demons, the comfort of pleasant thoughts. And you can't fall into the cave if you keep your eyes slightly open and your gaze turned inward. That, incidentally, is how Buddha's teaching began, long before Buddha – when the first human being first looked within.

Master Deshimaru once gave an interview on the martial arts, called "Life Is Combat," in which he talked about the importance of the eyes. He explained that when your opponent's eyes move, cloud over, or become hesitant, then the time has come to attack. You can see your opponent's weakness in his eyes.

One day at the dojo I watched a combat between two Kendo masters, one of whom was very old and ranked thirteenth *dan*. The two men squared off against each other. They didn't move. They just looked each other in the eye. In the end, the old man won. Hard to figure out why. It almost looked like they'd decided ahead of time.

Sometimes Master Deshimaru talked about not showing your weak points to others so that they can't take advantage of you. He didn't say it in a spirit of competition, the spirit of "Who's the strongest? Who's going to win?" That's just a false view of life. When Sensei talked about life being combat, he was talking about the meaning of life, about what life is. It's better not to count on others, not to put your faith in a human being. It's not fair to the human being in question. It's better to put your faith in the Dharma.

So Dogen tells us to always keep our eyes open. In zazen, if the back of your neck is straight and your chin is naturally pulled in, then your gaze will automatically fall a few feet in front of you, and you will look into yourself.

... breathe gently through your nose. In zazen, you should not make noise with your breathing. There's no need to take in a lot of air. It's not the quantity that's important, it's the depth. If you concentrate on breathing deeply, you won't make any noise. Breathe gently, imperceptibly, and you will free yourself from your chain of thought. Body will harmonize with mind, and mind with body, and wisdom will appear.

When you are in the correct posture,
take a deep breath in and out. Swing your
body left and right and settle into a steady posture.
Think not-thinking. How do you think not-thinking?
Beyond thinking – hishiryo.
This in itself is the essential art of zazen.

Hishiryo. Hi is a negation, but with an added sense of going beyond; *shiryo* is "thinking." That's the substance of zazen. Put a little more concretely, it's thinking not-thinking and not-thinking thinking. It's not a concept: it's action in the present moment, here and now. This is the zazen that we practice.

Here's a Japanese poem that expresses *hishiryo*:

The moon does not think to be reflected,
Nor the water think to reflect –
The lake of Hirosawa![1]

And here is another poem, this one by Master Daichi, which captures the essence of this passage of the *Fukanzazengi*:

What I Experience During Zazen
The mind is ku, the tranquil state.
The body is perfectly balanced.
It is like a solitary lantern
Shining in the sun.

The mind is *ku*: without substance, without any fixed form, without a soul. This is our real and deep nature, and it is of the same essence as the cosmos. My co-disciple, Michel Bovay, says that "in the tranquil state, your body becomes stable and perfectly balanced. In this state of stability and equilibrium, even if thoughts appear, the mind does not follow them." And in this perfect balance, you are like a lantern in the sun – meaning that you can let the light of zazen shine within yourself, here and now.

Chapter Three
Like the Tiger
Entering the Mountains

*The zazen of which I speak is not about
learning to meditate. It is none other than
the Dharma of peace and happiness, the
practice-realization of perfect awakening.
Zazen is the manifestation of ultimate reality.*

Zazen is not just some technique you learn. What is there to
learn, aside from pulling in your chin or stretching your back?
Despite what a lot of masters say – even Zen masters – there
are no steps, no progress, and no ranks. You don't go forward
and you don't go backward. You're just part of the cosmic order. In a lot of other Zen schools they use degrees and titles
the way you use a carrot to get the mule going. You practice
ten years and you're a taiko; after twenty, you get to be a *godo*
or a *roshi*. And then there's the first-degree *shiho*, the second-
degree *shiho*, and so on and so forth. Okay, maybe that's the
way it works, but looking back from the grave, all that isn't
very important.

We say that zazen practice itself is satori. That idea became one of the pillars of Master Dogen's teaching, which he developed in his *Seven Principles of Zen*. It's very deep and not easy to understand with your head. I think that we can only understand it after years of zazen. Because even though zazen is satori – as we are told by Dogen and all the masters of the tradition – that doesn't mean that you can obtain satori by practicing zazen. Anyway, who is it that has satori?

When I arrived at the Pernety Dojo in Paris in 1972, I sat down in the posture and saw others sitting in it, and I said to myself, "There it is! That's not thinking! It's not the head, or ideas, or concepts. It's not perception or sensation. It's not what you can see, hear, smell, touch, taste, or think. It's action in the here and now." And I wasn't wrong. Later, when I met my master and started to learn the teaching and understand it in my gut, I realized that this is one of the central themes of Buddhist practice.

Never think that zazen is passive. It's perfect activity – that is, if you don't follow your thoughts or fall asleep. You breathe out slowly and deeply and you don't stagnate in random thoughts. It doesn't matter whether the thoughts are good or bad. If your body starts to slump down on the zafu, you stretch your back. When your hands slide forward, you pull them back against your lower abdomen. When your chin falls forward, you pull it in and stretch the back of the neck.

Dogen tells us that *zazen is the manifestation of ultimate reality*. Reality can't be anywhere but here, right where you are. Reality isn't yesterday or tomorrow. That's illusion. Reality is a succession of heres and nows. Reality is what is. It is original nature.

Hanshan was a Chinese poet who practiced zazen in the 7th century. As is often the case in Buddhist history, he took his name from the mountain where he lived. Here is a poem by him about reality in which he talks about the mountain, the valley, himself and finally, the present moment:

Strange is the way that leads to Hanshan.
No ruts or hoof prints can be seen.
Valley winds into valley, peak rises above peak.
The grass sparkles with dew, and the pines whisper in the wind.
Don't you understand?
Reality asks the shadow for directions.

Traps and nets can never touch it. When you have touched its heart you are like the dragon entering the sea and the tiger entering the mountains.

There are so many traps in life and in spiritual practice: word traps, sutra traps, Bible traps, Koran traps; personal love traps, ambition traps, jealousy traps, comparison traps; even in zazen, there are wanting-to-get-something-out-of-it traps and category traps. Our practice is to face up to these things and recognize them for what they are – *bonnos*, illusions, nets we make for ourselves out of our own dualistic thinking. That's why Zen teaching says things like, "On the Way there is neither north nor south." When we think "north" or "south," or that Bodhidharma came from the "west," we're creating categories.

These traps and snares can never touch zazen, when it is practiced correctly. But they do lie in wait – even for tigers and dragons.

The dragon and the tiger are well-known Zen images, symbols of great disciples and monks. Dogen is saying that when you practice deeply, you find your true home. In order to do that, you must not create any distance between yourself and what you're doing right now. It's not a cerebral thing. It's the work of body and mind together, *tanden*.[1]

The dragon lives in the water, but he sometimes travels in the clouds, and when he does, he's cold. The dragon is also mortally threatened by the *garuda*. Sometimes he feels alone, lost and unhappy – the way I sometimes saw Master Deshimaru feel. But when the dragon (or the master, or the disciple) returns to the great ocean (zazen) he finds his natural, original home. He shakes off the nets and becomes free, strong, and peaceful again. It's the same for the tiger: he doesn't always feel perfectly at home either. But when he returns to the forest, he returns to his natural condition – true intimacy – and he is not influenced by the ten thousand external phenomena.

The truth, and our natural home, lies in simplicity, and nowhere else.

> **Understand that at this precise moment the real Dharma is manifested and that, from the beginning, physical and mental weakness and distraction are cast aside.**

A few paragraphs back, Dogen described how to get into the posture; later he will describe how to end *zazen*; here, he is talking about the "precise moment" when we are doing zazen, the moment the real Dharma is manifested. In this context, *Dharma* means "truth," "universal principle," or "cosmic order." Why does it manifest? Simply because it isn't your individual self sitting there facing the wall. It's not Mr. X or Ms. Y. In ordinary situations, when you aren't concentrating, naturally and unconsciously you know who you are. When you're exercising, you know who you are. When you're in a meeting or listening to a lecture, you know who you are. But when you sit in zazen, the idea of the self, the individual, doesn't exist. So who is sitting there?

That's when the Dharma is manifested. Because at that moment there is no separation between the Dharma, zazen, and your original nature. If you can understand that deeply, with your mind and your body, then the Dharma will manifest itself within you, not only in the dojo but everywhere, all the time, in all situations.

One of the koans that you often hear – Jack Kerouac even cites it at the beginning of *The Dharma Bums* – is, "Why did Bodhidharma come from the West?" (To which, in Kerouac's book, the old cook replies, "I don't care.")[2] That means, what did Bodhidharma bring from India to China? The short answer is: nothing. Why? Because the Dharma was already there, and his teaching consisted in showing people that the Dharma exists everywhere.

Of course, everybody's different. So the practice of the Dharma is different for each of us, depending on our individual situations. There's not just one style. However, in order for the Dharma to be manifested, continuous, increasing practice is essential. And any discussion that takes place before a real quest for the Way has begun is useless.

So Dogen says that when you have touched the heart of zazen – that is, when you are sitting in the correct posture with the correct mental attitude – then there is no more weakness or distraction. In Zen we call these states *kontin* – sluggishness, dulled consciousness, physical and mental fatigue – and *sanran* – dispersion, distraction, lack of concentration. These two states are obstacles to the practice of the Way. Everyone tends to fall into *kontin* or *sanran*. Early on in my own practice, I would often sleep during zazen; then I went through a long period of being unfocused and distracted, always thinking. This is the accumulated past of the unconscious rising to the surface and coming out in zazen. But with continued practice, these states can disappear completely. This is one of the benefits of zazen.

There are ten "infinite merits" of zazen; though they may seem to happen over time, we could also say that they occur in the "precise moment" that Dogen is talking about:

1. The five sense organs return to their condition of spiritual peace.
2. The mind is purified.
3. Illusions fade and disappear.
4. The mind of attachment is weakened.
5. External influences and stimuli lose their strength.
6. The four minds vanish; fear disappears.
7. The mind of compassion opens.
8. The power of patience increases.

9. Wisdom appears.
10. Faith deepens; the religious mind reveals itself.

When we are in this posture – which includes the perfect posture of the body; deep, slow breathing; and a mind that fixes on nothing – today, just as two thousand years ago, how could the Dharma not be manifested at this precise moment?

> **When you get up, move easily,**
> **without haste, calmly and deliberately.**
> **Do not stand up suddenly or brusquely.**

The way you get up after zazen is important. First you put your hands on your knees and make a fist around your thumb. (This is a *mudra* that represents peace; the thumb outside the fist represents violence, aggression, or self-defense.) Swing your upper body from right to left. Breathe deeply once or twice. Then stand up and press your zafu back into shape by pushing it against the floor with your hands. At the same time stretch your knees. That's important, especially if your legs hurt. Of course, you should get up neither too quickly nor too slowly.

Usually, after about thirty minutes of zazen, we stand up to do a walking meditation called *kinhin*, which lasts for five or ten minutes. Then we return to our places and begin zazen again.

When zazen is over, it's obviously not a good idea to be in a hurry or to start talking right away. It's good to remain quiet and calm, as much as possible. That's not hard if you're going home right after zazen. But in our sangha in Europe, for example, when we're all practicing together at La Gendronnière Temple, or in a dojo, we often eat together after zazen, or have a drink. Then it's hard not to start talking – in fact, we excite one another.

Personally, I don't think that's so bad. It's the joy of zazen, the free expression of our zazen at work.

This kind of expression is frowned upon by many Soto Zen institutions. In Japan, in the United States, and now in Europe, the norm is no alcohol, no meat, no cigarettes, no talking. But I think we have to be careful about not locking ourselves into ready-made ideas about what religion should be like. The main rule is not to disturb the atmosphere in the dojo. One of the rules Master Dogen set for his first temple was, "Don't enter the dojo drunk; if you do so by accident, you should repent." Perhaps, they weren't as strict back then as some people would like us to believe.

When we look at the past we see that transcending both awakening and non-awakening, dying while sitting or while standing, has always depended on the strength of zazen.

Here Dogen is talking about looking back at the example set by historical masters, masters who transcended the sacred and the ordinary.

Bodhidharma, for example, was once questioned about his practice and satori by the Emperor Wu. He answered by saying, "*Kakunen musho.*" *Kakunen* means "open sky" or "infinite heaven"; *musho*, says Sensei, means "no holiness, no madness." I like the juxtaposition of holiness and madness, because they seem such opposites in our illusory world, when actually, as Bodhidharma points out, they're not so far apart at all. No holiness, only the immensity of the sky. In order to discover that, you have to open up and take off the roof.

Thanks to the power of zazen, masters not only transcended the sacred and the ordinary: some of them actually died in zazen or *kinhin*. For example, Mahakashyapa, Buddha's first disciple, died on Mount Kukku seated in zazen. Almost the entire lineage of early patriarchs in China died that way: Bodhidharma was poisoned but he managed to get into the posture to die; Eka didn't have time to sit down – he was murdered in the street by rival Buddhists. So there you are: Buddhism isn't as pure as people sometimes say. Nothing is.

Doshin died in zazen. Konin died in zazen. Eno, the sixth patriarch, died in zazen. There is a famous passage where he says to his disciples, "Now I'm going to die." Then he sits down in zazen and dies. Sosan, the author of the *Shinjinmei*, died in *kinhin*. Sozan, who wrote the *Go-i*, died doing *gassho* under a tree. Master Shikan died standing up. Bassui of the Rinzai tradition died in 1387 in Japan. He sat down in zazen and said to his disciples, "Don't be fooled (by your illusions). Watch closely. What's this?" And he died. He was sixty years old.

There was even a master who died standing on his head. His sister, a nun, found him that way in the dojo. She came back an hour later and he was still on his head. She realized he was dead and pushed him, saying, "Stop showing off!" Then he fell down.

The way these masters died isn't something special or supernatural. It's the unconscious use of the force, power, and vigor of zazen. What's important is not that they died in zazen, but that, thanks to their constant practice and their karma, they were able to die naturally, the way they had lived.

Moreover, it is impossible for the dualistic mind to understand the possibility of enlightenment in the occasion provided by a finger, a flag, a needle, or a mallet, or the attainment of understanding thanks to a hossu, a fist, a stick, or a shout.

The items in this list refer to specific stories in Buddhist history – most of which can be found in the *Mumonkan* and *Hekiganroku* – which show masters going beyond words to express the vastness of the teaching. Here Dogen seems to be in favor of these different methods used to awaken disciples; but later he would criticize this sort of Zen education, which is particularly associated with the Rinzai School.

... a finger ...

A nun once asked Gutei, "What is the essence of Buddhism?" He didn't know what to say, and the nun went away quite disappointed. Later, when his master, Tenryu, visited him, Gutei asked him the same question: "What is the essence of Buddhism?" Tenryu silently held up his thumb. Gutei had satori. He understood that the essence of Zen was beyond words. Later Gutei became famous for teaching with his thumb. When he couldn't answer a question with words – what is *ku*? What is *mu*? What is satori? – he would hold up his thumb.

Gutei had a boy attendant who began to imitate him. Whenever a visitor asked what his master had taught that day, the boy raised his thumb. Gutei heard about this, seized the boy, and cut off his thumb with a knife. As the boy ran screaming from the room, Gutei called to him. When the boy stopped and turned, Gutei held up his thumb. In that instant the boy had satori. Personally, I think I'd rather keep my thumb than have satori, but you never know.

When he reached the end of his life Gutei said, "I received the one-finger Zen from Tenryu. I used it my whole life and never wore it out." Then he held up his thumb and died.

... a flag ...

Some translations of the *Fukanzazengi* use the word "pole" instead of flag. It is said that Ananda, the second Buddhist patriarch, realized the truth when he saw and heard a pole fall at a temple.[3]

Master Sekiso said, "You are at the top of a one-hundred-foot pole. Now you must take another step." Another master said the same thing somewhat differently: "One who sits atop the one-hundred-foot pole has not quite attained true enlightenment. Take another step from the top of the pole and throw your body into the one hundred thousand universes."

... a needle ...

Buddha's disciple Annirhuda was always falling asleep when Buddha was teaching. Appalled by his own laziness, he vowed never to sleep again, and began working day and night without rest. Buddha told him several times that while a monk should not be lazy, working excessively without rest was also an error. Annirhuda replied, "I cannot forget the vow I made." Eventually, he went blind. One day, he was trying to mend his kesa but could not thread the needle himself. The Buddha heard about this and came to see him in his hut. "Annirhuda," he said from the doorway, "give me your needle and thread, and I will mend your robe." The old monk recognized his master's voice and asked, "You have practiced compassion and good deeds for so long – why have you come to help me thread this needle?" Buddha told him, "Like you, I cannot forget the vow I made." At that Annirhuda had satori.

... a mallet ...

It is said that the Bodhisattva Manjusri, known for wielding a sword in order to cut karma, sometimes brandished a mallet to teach the Dharma.

There is also the case of Kyozan, who dreamed he went to Maitreya's Pure Land and sat in the third seat. A monk there struck the wood with a mallet[4] and said, "Today the one in the third seat will give a sermon." Kyozan arose, also struck the wood with the mallet, and said, "The truth of Mahayana is beyond any verbal expression! Listen, listen!"

... a hossu ...

A *hossu* is a stick about twelve inches long with yak hair at one end. It started out as a fly swatter, but later became a symbol of the transmission from master to disciple, and now is basically a ceremonial object. In our lineage, the master carries a hossu during the ordination ceremony. It's also used to keep off human pests. The hossu should not be confused with the kotsu, which is a short curved stick that the master carries in the dojo. It's a symbol of authority.

Baso asked his disciple Hyakujo: "How would you teach others?" Hyakujo raised his hossu. Baso said, "Is that all? No other way?" Hyakujo threw the hossu down.

... a fist ...

Dogen is perhaps alluding to the story of Rinzai, Taigu, and Obaku, one of the most famous satori stories in the history of Zen.

Rinzai had been following Master Obaku's teaching for three years, but he'd never asked him a question. One day Obaku's *shusso* encouraged Rinzai to go and ask something of the master. "Ask him, 'What is the essence of Buddhism?'" he suggested. Rinzai did as he was told, but each time he asked the question, Obaku merely whacked him repeatedly with the *kyosaku*. After the third time, Rinzai had had enough. He asked if he could leave for a while. The *shusso* gave him permission, but said he must be sure to visit Master Taigu (whose name means "Great Fool").

"Why are you here?" Taigu asked Rinzai when he showed up.

Rinzai explained all that had happened, and finished by asking, "So please tell me: what is the essence of Buddhism?"

"Obaku has treated you with grandmotherly kindness," answered Taigu. "He gave you the exact answer to your question. You're foolish and your head is thick."

Rinzai had satori at that moment. Taigu told him to return to Obaku, which he did. He went directly to the master's room.

"Well," said Obaku, "look who's back. Do you understand the essence of Buddhism now?"

"Yes, I understand it completely," said Rinzai, and punched Obaku.

"Go back to the dojo," said Obaku. "And next time, be careful not to touch the tiger's whiskers."

Joshu went to a hermit and asked, "What's up?" (In other words, "What can you teach me?") The hermit held up his fist.

Joshu said, "The water is too shallow to anchor here," and went away. A few days later, Joshu visited the hermit again and said, "What's up?" The hermit raised his fist again. Then Joshu said, "Well given, well taken, well killed, well saved." And he bowed to the hermit.

... a stick ...

This is surely a reference to the *kyosaku*, or "wake-up stick," which came into use in the 9th century, in Master Seppo's time. It continues to be used today in some lineages, including the Deshimaru sangha, where it is much respected. But in Japan and the United States, the tradition of the *kyosaku* is fast disappearing: dojos in the Suzuki, Uchiyama, and Kennett lines, among others, forbid its use.

There's a famous story about Master Tokusan and his fondness for the kyosaku. He once held it up to his disciples and said, "If you call this a stick: thirty blows. If you say it is not a stick: thirty blows. So: what is it?"

... a shout.

Baso was known for shouting. One day he screamed so loudly that his disciple Hyakujo was deaf for several days. Master Rinzai was also famous for his shouting. Usually a monk would ask, "What is the essence of Buddhism?" and Rinzai would scream "KWAAAT!" (an exclamation with no particular meaning). Then the monk would bow in *gassho*.

The writer Charles Bukowski once said, "If you can't say it with words it's because what you have to say isn't valid." This is not really the Zen approach. Shouts and blows were meant to shake up the mind and push it out of its dualistic thinking. If you're focused on your ego, you're automatically in a dualistic state of mind. And words are often a trap that keeps us in duality. However, we shouldn't think that words are an obstacle to satori, or that awakening happens in zazen.

Master Deshimaru once asked me to be the official note-taker during our summer retreat, and to write down everything he said in the dojo. We were alone, going up the stairs of the main house in the temple. "Sensei," I complained, "I don't want to take notes. I want to do zazen." He turned to me and said, "Zazen not important."

Everyone who knew Master Deshimaru was touched by something he said or did. Those experiences are personal, but the master isn't personal. He's universal. It is in the meeting of personal and universal that awakening, understanding, and realization can occur. And this meeting, this exchange, cannot be a simple imitation of tradition. Many masters since Gutei and Rinzai have held up their thumbs or yelled "*Kwaaat!*" But it's false. You can't copy that kind of thing. You can't explain Buddhism using Tokusan's stick or Baso's shouts, or by borrowing Dharma expressions. It's not the form that counts; it's sincerity. There's nothing to imitate, nothing to borrow. Through this practice we learn to create. Whatever the dualistic human mind might think, it is possible for ten thousand dharmas to be realized on the tip of a finger.

In truth, it cannot be better understood through the use of supernatural powers. It is beyond what human beings can see or hear – is it not a principle which precedes knowledge and perception?

No supernatural power will help us to understand the awakening that may be caused by a raised thumb or a *hossu*. No supernatural power will help us to understand *bodaishin* – the mind that sees the impermanence of the world, the impermanence of birth and death. The power of zazen here and now is natural, and through that natural power we can see our real nature, which no supernatural power can show us.

Supernatural powers do exist. It is possible, through constant practice, to see the past and the future, to bring forth demons, ghosts or spirits and make them visible. Through rigorous training, day after day and year after year, with a view towards developing supernatural powers, consciousness grows to a point where one can see what was hidden. There is a practice called *ninjitsu*, based on correct breathing, which allows one to become invisible at will. These things are only magic powers, and the people who practice them do not abandon their false ideas and illusions. Their supernatural accomplishments don't help them to enter the Way of awakening, the way of the buddhas, the way of great freedom.

We don't teach these supernatural practices in our sangha. Real magic begins with the natural power and energy of the buddhas and bodhisattvas.

Gozu was a disciple of Master Doshin and he founded a lineage that lasted for some two or three hundred years and ended with master Dorin, the master who lived in a tree. But before he met Doshin and started doing zazen, Gozu lived for some twenty years alone in the mountains. He observed an extremely ascetic discipline. He didn't eat meat or drink alcohol. He lived in a cave and enjoyed a very special relationship with animals. Birds in particular looked after him, bringing him flowers at mealtime. He was also close to tigers and wolves, who took turns protecting him and his cave.

One day, Master Doshin decided to pay a visit to Gozu. When he arrived at the cave in the mountains, he saw the tigers and pretended to be afraid. Then he just walked past them and entered the cave. Gozu was surprised. He said, "Are you always like that?" Doshin answered, "Like what?" Now, this exchange might seem very ordinary; but if you look at it closely you will find infinite meaning. It's all about *mushin* – no mind, nothing fixed in the mind.

Gozu had a great satori at that moment. After that the birds didn't bring him flowers anymore and the tigers and wolves went off to the forest and left him. He lost his supernatural powers and everything returned to the normal condition, which is the beginning and end of our practice. It's the original condition.

Here is a poem by Master Tozan:

Beyond ku
Beyond mu
If you want extraordinary things
Go home and sit in the ashes.

Tozan goes home, sits down in the ashes, and creates from within, from *mu*, from nothing. "In the ashes" means that thoughts, ideas, opinions, attachments, problems, and desires have fallen away, like a bare tree when the leaves have fallen. Perhaps great artists create from that point; authentic masters certainly do. And there's nothing supernatural about it.

Here is a *mondo* that dates back about eleven centuries; that is to say, about two hundred and forty years after Gozu met Doshin:

A monk asked Joshu, "Why did the birds stop bringing flowers to Gozu after Doshin came to see him?"

It's a good question. I could have asked it myself at the beginning of my practice. Why is it that Gozu lost his magic powers when he became Doshin's disciple? I heard Joshu's answer in a kusen once and it struck me deeply. Sometimes you hear something and the circumstances – the silence in the dojo, the kusen, your state of mind – cause it to go straight to your heart. In my case I read and re-read the exchange between Joshu and the monk. The more you read something – read it slowly and look at each word – the deeper it becomes.

Joshu's answer was, "One gets tired of gathering firewood and fetching water."

Magic is limited because it is merely personal. The body and mind of zazen is universal. It was there before birth, and it continues after death. If you are deeply concentrated and someone asks, "Who are you?", you find it hard to answer, hard to know, because there is nothing personal then.

Generally speaking, when we die our mind follows our karma, our strongest desires and attachments, our personal loves and hates. This is called transmigration, or *samsara*, the process of endless birth and death, depicted in Tibetan Buddhism as the Wheel of Life. There are animals, *devas* (gods), warriors, human beings, *gakis* (hungry ghosts), and beings in hell. The individual person is stuck on this wheel. Maybe he's killed someone and now he's in hell, or he's been stingy and mean so now he's a *gaki*, or else he's ignorant like a beast or violent like a warrior. None of these conditions is really any better than the others. Even the gods are in the cycle of *samsara*.

Life and death. We float together, then we sink, we die. Then it starts again. The most extraordinary supernatural powers are ridiculously inadequate when it comes to breaking free of the cycle of transmigration. When it's time to die, the power of zazen – the power to let our last thought flow out to the universe – will allow us to go where we want. I like the way Master Deshimaru put it. He said, "At that moment, our imagination can touch the heart of the cosmos."

The Tibetans prepare for death with visualizations and mantras. That way, when you're dying and you go through *bardo*, you can, if you've learned your lesson well, go through unscathed. We don't think that way. We're not getting ready for anything. One of the underlying ideas in the *Fukanzazengi* is no steps, no degrees. That's *hishiryo*-thinking.

The awakening that Dogen is talking about goes beyond the sights and sounds of the world. It is beyond what we can perceive with our senses; it is not accessible through study or analysis. We cannot grasp it in an ordinary human way. It is a matter of faith: not Christian faith or Buddhist faith, but the faith that precedes religion, the faith that existed before there were monks, nuns, and bodhisattvas.

There are all sorts of faith: lukewarm faith – believing a little, but not too much; faith in the master but not in the practice – or vice-versa, faith in zazen but not in the master; faith in Buddhist teaching. And then there is faith that comes from the universe itself, a faith that recalls Shakyamuni, who became awakened when he saw the morning star.[5] This faith comes from outside of you. It's not something you make up in your head all by yourself. It's not a question of God either.

Not long ago there was an interesting news story about a sailor who was crossing the Pacific Ocean on a freighter. He was at the bow of the ship when he was overcome by a wave and thrown overboard. It was dark out and no one noticed that he had fallen into the sea. It wasn't until nine hours later that his cabin-mate realized it and informed the captain. Nine hours is a long time. But the captain decided to go back to see if they could find him, or what was left of him...if he hadn't been eaten by sharks! Miraculously, eighteen hours later, they found the sailor. He was floating on the waves, sleeping peacefully atop the swells. They woke him up with the foghorn. He opened his eyes and saw the boat. They threw him a ladder and he climbed onto the bridge.

"How did you do it?" asked the captain.

"Since I couldn't get anywhere by swimming," replied the sailor, who was, obviously, in the middle of the ocean, "I decided there was nothing to do but float on my back and give myself over completely to the powers of the ocean."

That's the way we should do zazen: naturally, automatically, and unconsciously.

Faith does not depend on practice; but faith is essential power. As Dogen says, it is a principle that *precedes knowledge and perception.*

When you do zazen, you should be like that sailor floating on the water. He's dead, and that's why he lives. That's how it is in the dojo. We don't move and we don't follow our thoughts. Eyes, ears, and tongue are still. We even wear black – we're all ready for the grave, all laid out in the coffin. Kodo Sawaki said that zazen is like looking at things from the point of view of the coffin. That's the perspective that allows us to float on the ocean of energy, the *kikai tanden.*

But this stillness, this "death," doesn't mean we reject or deny our senses. Many other religions promote this kind of moralistic, ascetic practice, but it's not the Zen way. Instead, we observe how dependent we usually are on our six senses: sight, hearing, smell, taste, touch, and thought.

The mind is our sixth sense organ, directing and controlling the other five: the hungry, searching, small, individual mind that uses the other senses as tools. We are so caught up in our sense impressions and our ideas and the conclusions we draw from them that our heart gets lost. And by "heart" I mean our nature, both individual and universal.

During zazen it's easy to not use your eyes, ears, nose, mouth, hands, and mind. You don't really need your senses in the dojo. But it's harder in daily life. A mouth tasting food may become the mouth of greed. Eyes looking at a man or a woman may become the eyes of sexual obsession. Ears that perk up to overhear a conversation may become the ears of anger.

But naturally and unconsciously we can break free of our six sense organs and their objects. How? Simply by breathing calmly, deeply, and unconsciously. That's why we say that your ears should be lined up with your shoulders, that your nose should be vertical and your eyes horizontal. With your head still and firmly on top of your body, the mind grows clear and wisdom arises. And it's the same in everyday life. You have to know yourself and not let yourself be taken in. It's not a question of denying your senses, but of finding deep freedom.

However, it does not matter whether
you are intelligent or not. There is no difference
between the dull and the sharp-witted.
When you concentrate your effort with
one-mindedness, that in itself is negotiating the Way.
Practice-realization is naturally pure.
Going forward is a matter of everyday living.

Being smart or slow, superior or inferior, doesn't count at all when it comes to practicing the Way. The deep meaning of zazen cannot be grasped by intellectual activity. It's beyond thought and sense perception. Everyone can practice, even an idiot. You often hear people say, "I'm not ready." That's silly. Everyone's ready. If you've got two legs and you can fold them, then you're ready. You don't even need two legs! You just need a body, that's all.

The highest truth exists in your body here and now. So don't follow abstract ideas. Follow your body.

Of course, it's important to be intelligent in some situations: if you want to become a general or a scholar, for example. But in the world of *hishiryo*, intelligence doesn't really matter. Kodo Sawaki says that it's better to be stupid than to be smart, because a smart person is just someone who doesn't realize how stupid he really is.

Also, so-called stupid people can do zazen without doubting, which is important in Soto Zen. Rinzai Zen is different: doubt and intelligence are considered important. For those of us who truly follow the Soto line, real practice starts when we leave our doubts behind. We have no doubts about zazen. To do zazen without doubting is to enter rapidly onto the Way. The intelligent person who has doubts, who thinks too much, who is constantly weighing the pros and cons, advances very slowly. It often happens that he only advances to a certain point before falling back because his head is too heavy with thoughts.

In Shakyamuni's time, people measured intelligence in terms of the ability to remember things. They remembered what Buddha said, and that's why we have the sutras. Back then Buddha had a disciple named Culapantaka who was completely stupid. In a previous life he had made fun of a monk who was very dull, and so he was reborn a dullard in Buddha's time. He couldn't remember anything. So Buddha gave him a broom and said, "Just sweep up! Don't do anything else!" By the continual, one-minded act of sweeping, Culapantaka became an arhat, the highest state in Hinayana Buddhism.

So progress – going forward – has nothing to do with being smart. It's an everyday thing. In this passage of the text, *everyday living* means the immediate, fundamental nature of each day. It's *genjo*, and *genjo* is the koan of day-to-day life or, if you prefer, the fundamental truth of our daily lives. Eating, sleeping, talking, going to the toilet, doing *gassho* before and after moving in the dojo: this is the stuff of awakening, of great freedom. No need to be smart.

Our practice of *shikantaza* has nothing to do with intelligence or its lack, because it has no goal. So there's no need to learn some special technique. There's no particular skill, aptitude, talent, competence, or qualification required. There isn't any hierarchy to advance in. You don't need to have the *shiho*, or be ordained, or wear a rakusu. All you need is a zafu and some courage. Why courage? Because it's not easy to come regularly to zazen, especially when you have problems. You have to find the courage to come and sit even when nothing and nobody encourages you to do so.

Master Deshimaru used to encourage us by saying that if we practiced zazen we would become great leaders. I can't say that. I would just say that it's a question of correct effort, the effort to go towards the truth by destroying everything produced in your head, because it's false, just so many illusions, *bonnos*. Destroy them with zazen, with the breath that levels all. And don't be discouraged when the illusions come back. That's the human condition.

Chapter Four
The Great Liberation

*On the whole, in this world and others, in India
and in China, the Buddha seal is respected.
The particularity of this school is simply devotion
to zazen, sitting still with complete commitment.*

Dogen wrote this version of the *Fukanzazengi* for the greater
public, beyond the clerical or monastic readership. In this
passage he presents the Soto Zen that he received from Master
Nyojo to people of all countries, all times, and all conditions. This
teaching is to simply sit with complete commitment: *shikantaza*.
Shikan means "only concentration"; *taza* is "correct sitting."

"To practice zazen with a master is to abandon body and
mind: *shikantaza*," Nyojo taught Dogen. "No burning incense,
no veneration, no chanting the name of Buddha Amitabha, no
sutra reading."

Here is a poem from Dogen's *Eiheikoroku* that describes the
joy and simplicity of this practice. Night sitting, or *yaza* in Japanese, was common in Dogen's era, though today it is usually only
practiced at certain times of the year.

Gathered for evening zazen, we see the morning come.
This is the best part and we have no desire to sleep.
Thus we understand bendo, the true practice of the Way.
The voice of the valley reaches my ears,
    the light of the moon reaches my eyes.
Concerning zazen, there is nothing to attend to.

Although it is said that there are as many minds as there are humans, everyone must practice the Way in the same manner: by practicing zazen.

We should all practice single-mindedly. If you concentrate on the posture, the breathing, and the mind, then that's the Way. Dogen says that's satori. There's no reason to go off looking for satori anywhere other than here and now. There is no separation between zazen and satori. One is already the other.

Although there isn't really any difference between a beginner on the Way and someone who has practiced for many years, we can say that for the latter even the distinction between zazen and everyday life disappears. Practice and satori follow us everywhere, inside or outside the dojo, wherever we go.

Why zazen? The *Fukanzazengi* explains that zazen is not only for each individual, but for civilization as a whole. When practiced correctly, zazen reduces and changes our karma, unconsciously and automatically. I think this is what Dogen had in mind. Zazen creates an inner revolution that lays the foundation for an authentic civilization.

Here is how Master Nishijima translates this passage: *Although there are myriad distinctions and thousands of differences, we should just pursue the truth through Zen balance.*[1]

Another way of saying the same thing might be, "You may have heard of distinctions and differences, but whatever you hear, just practice zazen with simplicity and sincerity and seek the truth."

Here's an anonymous poem that states it more simply:

The wild bird sings unconsciously,
The unconscious flower blooms.
On a moss-covered rock,
A man sits in zazen.

It's not about philosophy. Dogen is just asking us to do zazen, whether we're monks, nuns, lay people, gods, or demons.

Why give up the place reserved for you at home to wander the dusty realms of other lands?

This is an allusion to the parable of the lost son in the *Lotus Sutra*. Most students of Buddhism know the story. A king's son leaves his father's palace and becomes a vagabond, a drifter, and a beggar. In fact, he forgets everything about his past. The king sends messengers to tell the son that he should come home, but he refuses to believe that he even has a home, let alone that his father is the king. One day, without realizing it, he comes begging at his father's palace. The king sees him coming and instructs his servants to give him a good quantity of food. The beggar comes back the next day and once again he receives food. He thinks he's on to something. Little by little he begins to work in the kitchen of this wealthy household. He starts to think, "Maybe I could get to be the cook. Then I could eat as much as I want. Who knows? Maybe one day I might get to be the overseer..."

And so he starts to work his way up, as his father intended. In the beginning he's happy to eat the scraps from the king's table (his own father's table! But he doesn't realize that yet.). "What a bit of luck," he thinks. "I can even help myself in the pantry when no one's looking." Then one day he's told that he doesn't have to eat standing up. He can sit down at a table in a room apart. He is given more and more responsibility. Finally, he believes the king when he tells him who he really is: "You are my son and this palace is yours."

When I first read this story in the *Lotus Sutra*, I wasn't very impressed. I thought that the son had psychological problems – that he was lost in life because he was lost in his head – and that was the point of the story. Sensei helped me to better understand this remarkable parable, and today I take pleasure in reading it. It's a Mahayana parable that describes the difference between the practice of the small vehicle – practice for oneself – and that of the great vehicle – *mushotoku* practice, practice for nothing, with no goal or profit.

Most people practice for themselves, for their own personal advantage. Maybe that's not so when they're actually in the dojo, because we insist so much on the idea of *mushotoku*; but elsewhere I'm sure it's true. Beggar or prince, we're all out for ourselves, from early childhood right up to the end. In the same way, Hinayana practice is personal development for one's own benefit, step after step, feeding oneself like the beggar fed himself from the king's kitchen. In a sutra it is written that if you take the Hinayana way, you will advance step by step for 86,410 million steps. At that rate, it's hard to get ahead.

So, in this parable we see the son hanging around in different places trying to get enough to eat and refusing to understand that he already possesses the royal treasure – Buddha nature. He happily eats scraps from the king's table while plotting to get hired as a cook. In other words, he's out for himself, trying to advance his own interests step by step. Only after a long journey through time and life does he finally realize his true wealth, his true princely nature. He's not just the son of an ordinary king, but the son of king Buddha Shakyamuni, the king who works not for his own profit but for nothing at all – in other words, for all human beings.

Here are the conclusions we can draw from this story: first, don't abandon your real treasure, the inheritance left by your true father; second, you should become Buddha here and now; and finally, don't waste your time hanging around in the wrong places. As Dogen says, "For those who stop to graze along the road, it is difficult to reach the great Way."

One false step and you stray from the Way that is set out right before you.

A step is either false or it isn't. There's no "almost" or "close enough" when it comes to the present moment. You're either there or you're not. The slightest notion of right or wrong and you're lost and confused. A single drop of ink in a glass of water is enough to darken it. Right and wrong are close together. Hell is not far from heaven. We often say that there's no reason to choose or to reject. Chasing and avoiding is focusing on the branches. Don't waste time on the branches: go straight to the root, straight to the mind of the Way, because all the rest is only of secondary importance.

*You have had the unique chance to take human form.
Do not waste your time. You are contributing to the
essential work of the Buddha Way. Who could take
vain pleasure in the spark from a flint?*

It really is hard to be born human; everyone reading this book has taken human form. It's also hard to hear the truth, but you do hear it. It's hard to navigate the Way correctly, but when following a true practice, it's easier to be exact. It's not enough just to come and sit. The present moment must be complete and whole, like the sound of a snapping finger: Snap! Time becomes eternity – no birth, no death. This is natural, automatic, unconscious satori.

Dogen states very simply, *Do not waste your time.* This is almost identical to the end of the *Sandokai* by Master Sekito, which concludes with these words: "I humbly tell those who seek the Way not to waste the present moment."

Most people who practice zazen know how not to waste time, how not to lose the present moment. But if you tend to waste time in your daily life, then it's very hard not to continue wasting time in the dojo. If you spend your time watching sports on television, playing cards, going to the cinema, discussing, chattering on about useless things, then how could you do otherwise when you're in the dojo? You just park your body the way you park your car, and then go wandering off in your head, mumbling to yourself or snoring.

When my co-disciples and I started out in the practice – thirty years ago for some of us – we quickly learned what the Way is when you're in the dojo. With Master Deshimaru, we all had satori right away in the dojo. Then later, unconsciously, we brought that experience out into our lives. But if you let yourself get stuck there, in the phenomena of the day-to-day world, it's hard to bring the Way back into the dojo again. Even after twenty years of practice, you can get lost and forget why you're there. So pay attention, whether you're an experienced monk or nun or a complete beginner. In Japanese, "attention" is composed of two characters: "present" and "mind." Present mind. That's what's urgent. That's not wasting time.

A layman asked the famous monk Ikkyu for a calligraphy. Ikkyu wrote, "Attention." The layman wasn't happy. "That's it? Can't you write something else?" So Ikkyu wrote, "Attention. Attention." The man didn't understand. He wanted something better than that and he was, after all, ready to offer a handsome sum of money. So Ikkyu wrote, "Attention. Attention. Attention." The layman walked away furious, saying, "That's not profound at all. What does it mean, anyway?" Ikkyu said softly, "Attention means attention."

Once I received a letter from a practitioner who said that zazen was good for "soothing her karma." False. First of all, zazen is good for nothing; thinking that it might serve some purpose is totally absurd and shows a complete lack of understanding of what we do. Second, zazen does not soothe anything – especially not karma, which in any case is not to be soothed, but cut away. Anyone who practices correctly will not find themselves soothed; on the contrary, you are harassed by the practice, by the Way. But you come to the dojo. You question yourself, you put your ideas into question, you see that your thoughts are not so deep after all, you see your illusions and errors ... but there is no soothing. And you come to the dojo anyway.

Most of us are preoccupied with life like busy crickets or grasshoppers. That image comes from Dogen's *Eiheikoroku*. It means that we talk vainly, waste time, chase after money or whine because we haven't got enough of it, entertain ourselves with television. For those of us who practice zazen, who wear the kesa or the rakusu, that's the worst way to be. The majority of people spend their whole lives in such futility, and it's too bad. But for those who practice the Way, who have been ordained, there can be nothing sadder than to come to the end of life without having clarified the mind.

It is written in the *Shukke Kudoku* that those who live south of Mount Sumeru – in other words, human beings – are lucky for four reasons:

1. We can practice the Way.
2. We can hear the teaching of Buddha.
3. We can become monks or nuns.
4. We can have satori.

A lot of people don't understand that when they hear it. They think that you're supposed to practice like crazy everywhere all the time. *Genmai* at the dojo and *genmai* at home with the family. No alcohol. No sex. No cigarettes. No parties. Walking around all the time with a serious expression. But that's not it at all.

The samurai Miyamoto Musashi had a disciple who absolutely wanted to learn how to use the sword. Musashi started his training by having him cut wood every day for three years.

The young man wasn't happy and he complained. "Okay, if you're tired of cutting wood you can walk on the edge of the tatami." So for another year the disciple walked along the edge of the tatami from morning to night. He got tired of that and went to complain to the master, who said, "Come with me. I want to show you something." He took the disciple up to the edge of a high cliff over a deep gorge. A tree trunk had fallen in such a way as to form a rough bridge over the chasm. The samurai said, "Go on, cross over." The disciple was afraid. One false step and he would plunge into the abyss. Just then, a blind man came up and walked straight over to the other side, tapping with his cane.

The practice isn't about getting something or going somewhere. It's all about the present moment. You have to know how to use it. It's not an idea: it's living experience.

A master asks his disciple, "Where have you been?"

"I was in Seto," the disciple replies. Apparently Seto is pretty far away.

The master says, "You must have worn out a lot of straw sandals."

The disciple says nothing and the master sees that he doesn't understand the practice.

"Too bad about the sandals," he says. "They've been worn out for nothing."

**_Form and substance are like dew on the grass,
destiny like lightning, vanishing in a flash._**

"Form and substance" are the human body – that is, ephemeral. The time between birth and death is brief. "I haven't got time now to practice the Way. I have to work and then I have to look after my family." And then? The days and years go by and soon your life is over. Maybe by the end you've managed to put together some money, a social position, a title. The house is paid for and the kids have grown up. But were you born for that? Is that all? Is that what you live for?

Of course the ordinary mind wants those things. But that's no excuse. You can't say that you're not smart enough or rich enough or stable enough to practice the Way. The Way hasn't got anything to do with intelligence, bank accounts, diplomas, social rank, or marital status. You have to have heart to practice; that's all. You have to free your heart from the constraints put upon it by your mind.

You've heard all this, but you didn't take it seriously. Now it's too late: you're going to die. So you die with your heart still darkened because you haven't learned how to let the light in through the practice. You haven't learned how to look at your dark side. A heart can remain chained to false ideas for an entire lifetime, right into the grave.

Everything is *mujo*. When a master ordains a monk, nun, or bodhisattva, he reads a text that talks about the futility of building fine things such as "a pagoda of seven treasures higher than thirty-three heavens." Things like that aren't important. Don't pile up names and titles, money, babies, lovers, houses, cars. Tear it all down. Take it all away.

On the block of wood that is struck at the beginning and end of zazen, the *han*, is often written a line from the *Nirvana Sutra*: "If we do not solve the problem of our life and death here and now, when will we?" When you are sitting in zazen and you hear the *han*, you know zazen – like life – is almost over. That's probably why Master Deshimaru once said, "When you hear the wood you should fear the passage of time." At that moment we should forget everything, abandon everything. Because later, it will be too late. For those who walk on the Way, the spirit of the Way, *doshin*, comes first, and everything else is only of secondary importance. However, abandoning everything else doesn't mean quitting your job and leaving your spouse and children. It implies something light, clear, and unhindered. It means not dwelling on the surface of things. It means constantly examining and correcting your own practice.

So listen attentively to the *han*. It's talking to you. But most people don't even hear it because their minds are elsewhere. It is struck slowly at first – *tock ... tock ... tock* – and then faster and faster – *tock-tock-tocktocktocktock* ... Like life passing.

**I beseech you, honored disciples of Zen,
long accustomed to groping the elephant in the dark:
do not fear the true dragon.**

Don't be afraid to take the highest and widest possible point of view with every thing or person you meet, with every sentient or non-sentient being. Don't waste time *groping the elephant in the dark*.

Dogen is alluding here to a story from the *Nirvana Sutra*. A king had an elephant brought before a group of blind men and let them touch it. Then he asked them what they were touching. The answers were all very different, but each was the result of limited, ordinary experience. The blind men couldn't use their eyes, so they used their hands. But they couldn't grasp the whole elephant. So the man touching the trunk said it was a tube for water; the one touching the ear thought it was a fan; the one touching the leg thought it was a pillar; and the one feeling the back thought it was a throne. Each man's understanding was limited to the part he had touched. That's ordinary mind; it's not the highest point of view, Buddha's point of view. There is a big difference between Buddha's understanding of things and the ordinary understanding of things.

Forget the ordinary way of looking. Look through the eyes of awakening.

Frankly, this story doesn't really stand up to scrutiny if you think about it. After all, an elephant is a living animal. If a blind man touches an elephant, he knows that he's not dealing with a pillar or a fan or some other inanimate object. It's warm and it moves and it has a smell. You can't take stories too literally. Dogen is telling you that you've been groping in the dark. The time has come to see clearly – and to be unafraid of what you see.

If you look within yourself – into your darkened heart – you can understand and bring light to your personal darkness. Each of us has his or her dark places, though most people avoid them. Our work in Zen practice is to not avoid them. We're not here to analyze them, either. This isn't a doctor's office. You need the courage to go forward, to cut off the past and the future. Don't let your life go by without bringing light to your mind and, by so doing, lighting all minds.

I have often wondered how to see into the dark places of my heart. I forced myself to work on it, to try to see myself directly. It's very difficult. But I've come to understand that looking into your darkest places means becoming intimate with yourself. This is zazen, and through it you can find your real self, the true dragon, not the small, petty self. Why settle for an imitation?

In ancient China, a man named Sekko collected paper dragons. He loved them, and his room was full of them. One day a real dragon was passing in the sky – the sky being *ku*, emptiness – and thought he would make Sekko happy by dropping in. Wouldn't it be nice to show him a real dragon? So he stuck his head in the window. Sekko wasn't happy at all. He was so frightened that he fainted.

The dragon symbolizes reality – not a paper imitation. What is reality? It's your original nature. You might say that when you're in zazen, you are the dragon. Don't be afraid of zazen. Don't hide by sleeping or thinking. Don't hide by not-thinking either. Face the real dragon.

We've all met or heard of people who are afraid of sitting, afraid of coming face to face with themselves. For those who practice, this experience is essential; but for most people, it's daunting. It's not the physical pain of zazen that's frightening: it's what comes after the pain.

Devote your energies to the Way which points directly to the absolute.

Now that you have discovered the practice – and, through the practice, the Way – go straight on without turning left or right, without distracting yourself.

One day, a woman who had been practicing with me for years said she was leaving to follow a Vietnamese master because she didn't feel welcome in our sangha. It's true that Zen is cold. It's like snow. It's Eka cutting off his arm. But the heart is there. You just have to find it. If you want to look somewhere else – no problem. Do as you like. But where will you go after the next master, and the next school? Time is running out. Yesterday was yesterday but today I must die. Spend all your time looking for something new and you just might miss what's important. Don't waste time over details which, in the end, are only illusions anyway. Put all your energy, all your courage, your whole life into the Way.

Respect the realized person who is situated beyond human actions. Harmonize with the enlightenment of the buddhas; succeed to the legitimate dynasty of the patriarchs' satori. Always behave this way, and you will be like them.

What does it mean to be *beyond human actions*? The first verse of the *Shodoka* says:

Dear friend, can't you see
The man of satori who has stopped studying and acting?
He does not push away illusions and he no longer
seeks the truth.

People often misinterpret this to mean that they should stop studying the Way and become passive. But in fact it means moving beyond goal-oriented study and action; it means not trying to get somewhere; it means studying and acting in the sense of preserving and protecting the Dharma. As it is said at the beginning of the *Hokyozanmai*, "Now that you have found it, protect it well."

Don't fight illusions. Don't seek the truth. Don't fall into the subject/object trap. Don't put another head on top of your own. This is the action of all buddhas: the realization of the present moment. And when you do zazen, you are harmonizing with their enlightenment.

Here's a short poem that Dogen wrote in another context:

The wind sweeps away the clear and marvelous teaching
   of the patriarchs –
Ten million mountains and rivers rolling out to infinity.

At this very moment, the wind, the teaching of the patriarchs, is blowing, sweeping clean and smoothing our mind. The ten million mountains and rivers are the landscape of our life. These things are transmitted without transmission – that is, without language. They are the sounds of nature: the voice of the valley, the sermon of non-sentient beings, the owl hooting, and the cricket chirping.

When Master Dogen refers to *the legitimate dynasty of the patriarchs' satori,* he is talking about his own deeply intimate relationship with the ancient patriarchs, but also about *our* relationship with them, and with him. That intimacy still exists.

Now, here is the last sentence of the *Fukanzazengi*:

**Your treasure house will open of itself,
and you can use it as you wish.**

Those who find the secret of the patriarchs' satori are free, and may do as they wish with this treasure.

Master Deshimaru once asked me to re-translate these words from French into English. I took them home with me, and when I had finished studying them I was deeply moved. This vision of perfect freedom brought tears to my eyes.

This treasure is *jijuyu zanmai*: intimacy with yourself, with others, with the tradition.

It's nothing special.

It's the normal condition.

It's zazen.

Endnotes

Chapter 1

1. Master Deshimaru's first dojo in Paris opened on the rue Pernety in 1972. After his death, the Paris Zen Dojo (*Dojo Zen de Paris*) moved first to the rue des Cinq Diamants, then to the rue Keller, and finally to its current address on the rue de Tolbiac

2. In fact Dogen had separate encounters with two different tenzos in China; to facilitate the presentation and comprehension of the essence of these stories, the author has joined them into one.

Chapter 2

1. Cited in *Zen and the Ways* by Trevor Leggett (Boulder, Colorado: Shambhala, 1978), p. 196.

Chapter 3

1. See glossary, *kikai tanden*.
2. *The Dharma Bums* by Jack Kerouac (New York: Signet Books, 1959).
3. Here's another version of the story:
   > Ananda asked Mahakashyapa, "Buddha gave you the golden robe of the transmission. What else did he give you?"
   > Mahakashyapa said, "Ananda!"
   > "Yes!" answered Ananda.
   > "Knock down the flagpole at the gate!" said Mahakashyapa.
   > Ananda had satori.
4. See page 86-87 for a more detailed explanation of the wood being struck.
5. The planet Mercury often appears in the early dawn twilight as the brightest "star," low on the horizon. Shakyamuni's satori under the Bodhi tree is reported to have happened just before dawn at the moment he saw the morning star shining in the night sky.

Chapter 4
1. From a translation of the *Fukanzazengi* by Gudo Wafu Nishijima and Mike Cross on the Zen Occidental website (http://www.zen-occidental.net/texteszen/fukan-zazengi1.html).

Glossary

A

Arhat, lit. "worthy one." In early (Hinayana) Buddhism, the highest form a human being can reach, free from attachments and ready to leave *samsara*, the wheel of life and death, and to enter *nirvana*. Mahayana Buddhism perceives this state to be not yet perfect and prefers the ideal of the bodhisattva, who vows to put aside his own liberation and be reborn until all beings are saved.

B

Bardo, lit. "in-between state." In Tibetan Buddhism, a transition state between two incarnations. *The Tibetan Book of the Dead, Bardo Thödol*, describes a number of different in-between states; successful progress through these states at the moment of death can be achieved with the help of a trained guide.

Baso Doitsu (Ch., Ma-tsu Tao-i, 709 – 788). Great Chan master of the Tang Dynasty; disciple of Nangaku and master of Hyakujo; the first to use the rough-method technique of shouts and blows to awaken his disciples.

Bassui Tokusho (1327 – 1387). One of the most outstanding Japanese Rinzai masters. He spent a homeless, itinerant life refusing to take disciples until he was fifty years old, shortly afterwards becoming abbot of a monastery for the last ten years of his life.

Bendo, lit. *ben*, "to make an effort" or "pursue"; *do*, "the Way." Master Dogen usually used the word to mean the practice of zazen; the Bendowa ("Talk about Pursuing the Way") is the first chapter of the *Shobogenzo* and describes the practice of zazen.

Bodaishin. The mind which aspires to the Way, to the highest buddhahood; the mind which observes *mujo*, the impermanence of the world, birth, and death.

Bodhidharma (Jap., Bodaidaruma or Daruma, 470 – 543?). Indian monk, disciple of Prajnadhara (Jap., Hannyatara), who went from southern India to China, where he spent the last ten years of his life. He lived in a cave on the site of Shaolin Monastery, where he sat facing a wall for nine years; the first Chinese Zen patriarch.

Bodhi tree. Fig tree (*ficus religiosa*) under which Shakyamuni Buddha had the experience of awakening after forty-nine days of zazen. The tree currently venerated at the north Indian city of Bodh Gaya is believed to be the offshoot of an offshoot of the original Bodhi tree.

Bonno. Illusion, attachment; a product of personal consciousness. The vow to cut *bonnos* is one of the four great Bodhisattva Vows, chanted every morning after zazen:

> However innumerable the sentient beings, I vow to save them all.
> However inexhaustible the passions, I vow to extinguish them all.
> However immeasurable the dharmas, I vow to master them all.
> However incomparable the Buddha's truth, I vow to attain it.

Bovay, Missen Michel (b. 1944). Zen master, close disciple of Master Taisen Deshimaru; former president of the International Zen Association (AZI) in Europe; currently head of the Zurich Zen Dojo; received Dharma transmission from Okamoto Roshi in 1998.

Buddha Amitabha, lit. "Endless Light." Mahayana Buddha embodying wisdom and mercy; venerated by the Pure Land School of Chinese and Japanese Buddhism, in the belief that simply invoking this name can lead to rebirth in paradise.

Buddha nature. According to the Mahayana view, the true, immutable, and eternal nature of all beings. Since all beings possess Buddha nature, it is possible for them to realize satori and become a buddha, regardless of what level of existence they occupy.

C

Chan (Skt., *dhyana*; Jap., *zen*). Established in China by the Indian monk Bodhidharma in the sixth century, Chan (or Zen) is the teaching of Buddhism in its most naked, bare, unclad, pure sense; the Buddha's teaching transmitted from master to disciple.

D

Daichi Sokei (1290 – 1366). Japanese Zen master famous for his poetry. He became a monk under Kangan Giin, a disciple of Dogen, practiced with Keizan for seven years, and finally received the *shiho* from Meiho Sotetsu, a disciple of Keizan.

Deshimaru, Taisen (1914 – 1982). Disciple of Kodo Sawaki; Japanese master of Soto Zen who spent the last sixteen years of his life teaching in Europe; received monastic ordination, as well as the robe, bowl, and spiritual transmission, from Kodo Sawaki in 1965; founded more than a hundred dojos in Europe, North Africa, and Canada, as well as La Gendronnière Temple in the Loire Valley in France. According to temple records, he ordained more than five hundred monks and nuns, and more than twenty thousand people practiced with him at one time or another.

Deva (Skt., "shining one"). The Buddhist pantheon contains myriads of celestial beings and gods on various levels of form and formlessness, desire and freedom from desire.

Dharma. The universal truth, teaching, and Buddhist doctrine pronounced by Shakyamuni Buddha; the truth, ultimate reality, or universal order; phenomena, or manifestations of reality.

Dogen Zenji (1200 – 1253). Disciple of Chinese master Nyojo and master of Ejo; introduced Soto Zen to Japan and founded Eihei-Ji Temple in the northern mountains of Japan. Born into a noble family, he studied Rinzai Zen and the koan method for several years with masters Eisai and Myozen, then crossed the sea to China, where he met Soto master Nyojo. He practiced with Nyojo on Mount Tendo for three years before returning to Japan as the heir of Nyojo's Zen. His masterwork is the *Shobogenzo*, which contains the major part of his teaching. His poems are collected in the *Sanshodoei*, with the exception of the *Eiheikoroku* poems, which were reserved for his closest disciples and kept secret for many years.

Dojo, lit. "hall of the Way." In a temple it is a large hall where the monks and nuns practice zazen. Similarly, in an urban Zen center: a room large enough to hold all the practitioners seated along the walls, with an altar in the middle for burning incense.

Dorin, Choka (late eighth century). Zen master in Gozu's lineage, and the last of that line. He is known for living and practicing zazen in a tree.

Doshin (Ch., Tao-hsin, 580 – 651). Fourth Chan patriarch, disciple of Sosan and master of Konin; created a community of five hundred disciples on Mount Shuang-Feng, where he died in zazen.

Doshin, lit. "mind of the Way." The spirit of the Way.

E

Eiheiji. Along with Sojiji, one of the two central temples of the Japanese Soto School. Eiheiji is in the mountains on the northern side of Honshu. Dogen founded the monastery in 1244 in this cold and inhospitable region in order to escape from the intrigues of the capital. He died there in 1253.

Eiheikoroku. A large collection of poems and teachings by Dogen, for the most part recorded after he had moved to his new monastery, Eihei-ji, in the mountains of northern Japan. Less well known than the *Shobogenzo*, it contains Dogen's spiritual bequest to his closest disciples, poems which were kept secret for many generations after his death.

Eisai Zenji (also Myoan Eisai or Senko Kokushi, 1141 – 1215). Japanese master of the Rinzai lineage, disciple of Chinese master Hsu-an Huai-ch'ang (Jap., Kian Esho) and Dogen's master before Nyojo; founder of Shofuku-ji, the first monastery in Japan in which Rinzai Zen was practiced.

Eka (Ch., Hui-k'o, 487 – 593). Disciple of Bodhidharma and the second patriarch; master of Sosan. He reportedly cut off his arm and placed it before Bodhidharma as an expression of his desire to be accepted as a disciple.

Eno (Ch., Hui-neng, 638 – 713). The sixth patriarch. He arrived at Konin's temple on Mount Obai when he was twenty-four and left after only six months, having received the transmission from his master. For fifteen years he lived with fishermen and hunters, then taught the Dharma on Mount Sokei for thirty-six years until his death.

F

Fuse. A gift of any kind, be it money, time, food, material or immaterial, given unconsciously without the expectation of reward.

G

Gaki. Japanese expression for "hungry ghosts," poor creatures with an enormous hunger but no mouths to eat with.

Garuda. A mythical beast, half-man, half-bird.

Gassho. A gesture of reverence in which the hands are joined, palm to palm, about ten centimeters in front of the face, the tips of the fingers almost level with the nose, the forearms horizontal. The left hand symbolizes the spiritual or holy world, the right the material or phenomenal world. The hands thus joined symbolize the unity of spiritual and material, of sacred and profane, of man and the cosmos.

Gendronnière, La. Zen temple located in the Loire Valley in France, founded by Master Taisen Deshimaru in 1979. In addition to a two-month summer retreat and intensive sesshin in winter, spring, and fall, the temple hosts workshops, symposia, conferences and other activities focusing on Zen Buddhism. Above all, it is a practice centre dedicated to sesshin, daily zazen, and *samu*.

Genjo. The immediate manifestation of things as they are; the materialization of phenomena; the actualization of satori in our daily lives.

Genmai. Rice soup traditionally eaten after morning zazen.

Gion Shogi. "The True Rules of the Dojo's Essence," also known as "The Standards of Jetavana"; a short text by Master Fuyodokai (Ch., Furong Daokai, 1043 – 1118).

Godo. In a temple, the person who gives the teaching in the master's absence; in Master Deshimaru's sangha, the monk or nun who leads a sesshin or teaches in the dojo.

Gozu Hoyu (Ch., Niu-tou Fa-jung, 594 – 657). Disciple of Doshin and a co-disciple of Konin, the fifth patriarch. He created his own branch of Zen, "Gozu Zen," which continued to be taught for a century after his death, then died out. Author of "The Mind's Song," a long poem similar to the *Shinjinmei*.

Gutei Chikan (Ch., Chü-chih, ninth century). Disciple of Koshu Tenryu, from whom he inherited "raised-thumb Zen," which he taught all his life.

Gyoji, lit. *gyo*, "practice, action, behavior"; *ji*, "to maintain, to keep." Continuous or eternal practice without beginning or end; the uninterrupted sequence of meditation and activity; title of one of the *Shobogenzo* chapters in which Dogen uses the history of the patriarchs to teach correct behavior.

H

Han. Japanese for "wood." A piece of planed or carved wood which is struck with a wooden mallet to summon practitioners to zazen and to mark the end of a sitting period.

Hannyatara (Skt., Prajnadhara). Indian master of Bodhidharma.

Hanshan (dates unknown, ca. seventh century). A Chinese poet and hermit, lay practitioner of Chan (Zen). He became a favorite theme of Zen iconography in China and Japan as an example of the natural, uncluttered practice of the awakened layman.

Hekiganroku (Ch., Pi-yen-lu), lit. "Blue Cliff Record." One of the most important koan collections in Zen, along with the *Mumonkan*; composed in the first half of the twelfth century by Chan master Engo Kokugon.

Hettsu (also Houn Entsu; Ch., Fayun Yuantong, exact dates unknown). Master of Chang-lu Tsung-tse (Jap., Choro Sosaku; d. 1107) of the Unmon lineage, who in his *Zennen Shingi* quotes his master's disapproval of sitting zazen with eyes closed.

Hishiryo, lit. "beyond thinking." Unconscious doing; action in the moment; the secret, inexpressible essence of Zen. It is not the thought: "Ah, now I'm letting my thoughts go," but the letting go itself. This term appears for the first time in the *Shinjinmei*, the oldest Zen text. Together with *mushotoku* and *shikantaza*, *hishiryo* is one of the three pillars of Zen teaching of Dogen, Sawaki, and Deshimaru.

Ho. Japanese for "Dharma," the cosmic order.

Hokyozanmai (Ch., San-mei-ko), lit. "Samadhi of the Precious Mirror." Poem composed in the ninth century by Chinese master Tozan Ryokai which celebrates the true nature of all things; recited every day in Japanese

Zen temples; considered to be one of the founding texts of Soto Zen, along with the *Shinjinmei*, *Shodoka*, and *Sandokai*.

Hyakujo Ekai (Ch., Pai-chang Huai-hai, 720 – 814). One of the founding fathers of the Rinzai School; disciple of Baso and master of Obaku. Known today for, among other things, his celebrated *Shingi*, or monastic rules. One of the most outstanding Chan masters of the Golden Tang Dynasty, he taught the Buddha Dharma for forty years and had one thousand disciples, thirty of whom received his transmission.

I

Ikkyu Sojun (1394 – 1481). Rinzai master, poet, and calligrapher known for his eccentricity and iconoclasm. He called himself "Crazy Cloud" or "Blind Donkey," and claimed to prefer taverns and brothels to monasteries. In 1474 he was appointed abbot of Daitoku-Ji, the temple where he had practiced for ten years in his youth before opting for a life outside of monasteries. He once tore up his certificate of transmission and took great care not to name any successors.

Inmo, lit. "this," "that," or "thus." Related to "thusness," one of the central Buddhist ideas: the evident and indescribable character of things; term often used by Master Dogen and title of one of the chapters of the *Shobogenzo*.

I shin den shin, lit. "from mind to mind" or "from heart to heart." A fundamental notion in Zen which describes the transmission beyond writing and intellectual understanding; the common intuition between master and disciple of reality as it is.

J

Jijuyu zanmai, lit. *jijuyu*, "accepted or received by oneself"; *zanmai*, "samadhi" or "one-mindedness." The inner joy we feel when we become intimate with ourselves through the practice.

Jinshu (Ch., Shen-hsiu, 605 – 706). Disciple of Konin and co-disciple of Eno, the sixth patriarch; founder of the Northern School of Chan, which advocated a gradual approach to the practice and which survived for only a few generations after his death.

Joshu Jushin (Ch., Chao-chou Ts'ung-shen, 778 – 897). One of the greatest Chan masters; disciple of Nansen Fugan (Ch., Nan-ch'uan P'u-yuan), whom he followed for forty years.

K

Kai. Precept. In Zen, the ten *kai* are the rules of natural integrity which the disciple accepts from the master during the bodhisattva, monk, and nun ordinations.

Kakunen musho, lit. *kakunen*, "infinite sky"; *musho*, "nothing sacred" or "no madness." The Emperor Wu of the Liang dynasty had invited Bodhidharma to visit him after his arrival in China. Wu was a generous patron of Buddhism and, among other questions, asked what the supreme meaning of the sacred truth was. Bodhidharma replied, "*Kakunen musho.*"

Karma. Law of cause and effect; the logical sequence of human behavior (thoughts, words, actions) and its good and bad consequences. Karma encourages correct behavior through the awareness of the effects of our comportment on the phenomenal world, rather than by following a moral code or awaiting reward or retribution in heaven or hell. Both individual and collective karma exist, and both transcend birth and death. Each person's practice influences the karma of humanity as a whole.

Keitokuji. Temple on Mount Tendo near Shanghai. The temple of Wanshi Shogaku and, later, Tendo Nyojo, where Dogen practiced and studied after meeting the temple *tenzo*.

Keizan Jokin (1268 – 1325). Great Japanese Soto master who practiced under both Ejo and Gikai, two of Dogen's closest disciples. He founded Sojiji, one of the two main Soto temples, wrote the *Denkoroku*, and was responsible for the initial and widespread promulgation of Soto teaching throughout Japan. While Dogen is often portrayed as a stern father, hard and implacable, Keizan is usually attributed the role of a mother with a big heart.

Ken. Opinion or judgment.

Kensho, lit. "seeing nature." Equivalent to satori; used to describe the experience of awakening. In Soto Zen, *kensho* is used pejoratively to describe the (incorrect) idea of a personal enlightenment experience as the goal of Zen training. Soto Zen has no goal.

Kesa (Skt., *kasaya*), lit. "earth-colored." A patchwork cloak or wrap, traditionally going back to Shakyamuni Buddha's recommendation to his disciples for a monk's robe: they should gather bits of used and soiled material, even shrouds, wash them carefully, dye them and sew them together. Many statues and *thangkas* show the Buddha wearing a kesa. Monks and nuns usually receive a kesa when they are ordained. In the past, a master gave his own kesa to a disciple as a symbol of Dharma transmission, thereby naming the disciple his successor.

Kikai tanden, lit. *ki*, "energy"; *kai*, "ocean"; *tan*, "essence"; *den*, "field"; also known as the *hara*, the central energy point in the body, situated four finger breadths below the navel. The deep, unforced breathing practiced during zazen goes down into this energy center. It is considered the connecting point between human beings and the cosmos and so is an expression of the unity of body and mind.

Kimono. In Zen, a robe worn for the practice of zazen; useful for tucking in the legs and feet during meditation, thus ensuring warm feet and a cool head.

Kinhin. Slow-motion walk to the rhythm of one's breathing, practiced between long periods of zazen; zazen in motion. Useful for stretching the legs while continuing the practice of zazen-mind (lit. "awareness mind").

Koan. Originally, in China, a law or judgment handed down from public authorities; in Zen, a universal truth expressed by a phrase from a sutra or a master; a paradox that only intuition can resolve, which steadfastly defies logical analysis; used as part of formal education in Rinzai Zen as a means to push disciples past their limits and into enlightenment. Soto Zen, which places no value on special states and considers satori the normal condition, generally does not use koans in the formal sense in disciple training. Nevertheless, for both Rinzai and Soto, the koan represents the hidden, intangible aspect of reality.

Kolomo. A black robe with very wide sleeves and a wide hem worn by Zen monks and nuns over a white or grey kimono.

Konin (Ch., Hung-jen, 601 – 674). The fifth patriarch, master of both Jinshu and Eno, whose separate teachings founded the so-called Northern and Southern Schools of Chan respectively.

Ku (Skt., *sunyata*). Often translated as "void" or "emptiness," as opposed to *shiki*, "phenomena." It does not mean a vacuum in a physical sense, but is infinity, the unborn from which all things born and finite come, and to which they return. It is the origin, the common identity without which differences (phenomena) could not exist.

Kusen. Oral teaching given during zazen; a teaching *i shin den shin* which is addressed to the listeners' *hishiryo*-consciousness, without passing through the intellect. The kusen appears to be a specificity of the Kodo Sawaki/Taisen Deshimaru lineage: most other lineages prefer lectures (*teisho*).

Kyosaku, lit. "wake-up stick." Used during zazen to hit the trapezius muscles (between shoulder and neck) of practitioners disturbed by drowsiness or mental or physical agitation. The *kyosaku* is not a form of punishment but a way to help restore the normal condition.

M

Mahakashyapa (sixth century BCE). One of the principal disciples of Shakyamuni Buddha, known for his self-discipline and moral strictness. He assumed leadership of the sangha after Buddha's death. Considered the first Zen patriarch, he received the transmission when Buddha, surrounded by his disciples, silently turned a flower in his hand. No one reacted except Mahakashyapa, who smiled: an illustration of *i shin den shin*.

Manjusri, lit. "he who is noble and gentle." The bodhisattva of wisdom, one of the most important figures in the Buddhist pantheon. In statues he is depicted holding a scroll and wielding a sword, symbolizing the wisdom which dispels ignorance and cuts karma. In Zen dojos there is usually a Manjusri statue on the altar.

Milarepa (1025 – 1135). Considered the greatest saint of Tibet; disciple of the yogi Marpa, from whom he learned *mahamudra* – freedom from emptiness and *samsara*. He lived for nine years as a recluse in a cave in the Himalayas, wearing only a thin cotton covering and practicing the yogi technique of "inner heat."

Mondo, lit. "question/answer." Any form of exchange whose purpose is an attempt to understand the Dharma. When conducted in a dojo, *mondos* provide the opportunity to clarify questions relevant to existence and to the practice for the benefit of the entire sangha.

Mount Hiei. A temple mountain overlooking Kyoto; scene of the massacre of the Tendai soldier-monks by the armies of Oda Nobunaga in 1671.

Mount Sumeru. The "world mountain" of Indian cosmology, standing at the center of the universe; meeting place of the gods.

Mu. A particle denoting "nothing," "nothingness," or "no." It suggests absence rather than negation; found in Japanese expressions such as *mushotoku* ("no profit") and *mushin* ("no-mind"). Not to be confused with ku.

Mudra (Skt., "seal" or "sign"). Gesture with or position of the hands. The *dhyani* (Zen) mudra is practiced during zazen: the fingers of the left hand are placed on the fingers of the right, with thumbs touching to form an elongated oval space.

Mujo. Impermanence. Nothing stays as it is; the fundamental condition of all life. Observing and accepting *mujo* are essential to the practice of the Way.

Mumonkan (Ch., Wu-men-kuan), lit. "The Gateless Gate." One of the most important collections of koans in Zen, compiled by Mumon Ekai and published in 1229.

Musashi, Miyamoto (1584 – 1645). Said to be the greatest samurai and a master of the sword, he spent over forty years moving from battle to battle, war to war. He revolutionized sword tactics in Japan.

Mushin, lit. "no-mind" or "non-mind." No personal mind; no-thought; freedom from dualistic thinking.

Mushotoku, lit. *mu*, the negative prefix; *shotoku*, "to obtain," "to profit." Nothing to obtain; without aim, purpose, goal, or object. Expresses the philosophical essence of Soto Zen – to be without hope of attaining satori or becoming Buddha.

N

Nangaku Ejo (Ch., Nan-yueh Huai-jang, 677 – 744). Early Chinese master associated with the Rinzai lineage, though he lived a century before Rinzai. Disciple of Eno, the sixth patriarch; master of Baso.

Nensokan. Awareness of the moment.

Nishijima, Gudo Wafu (b. 1919). Contemporary Zen master, student of Kodo Sawaki; ordained by and received Dharma transmission from Niwa

Zenji, the former abbot of Eiheiji; translator of a definitive, modern English version of Dogen's *Shobogenzo*.

Nyojo (Tendo) (Ch., T'ien-t'ung Ju-ching, 1163 – 1228). Chan master of the Soto School, disciple of Setcho Chikan and master of Dogen Zenji. He traveled from dojo to dojo, coming into contact with the many types of Zen existing in his time: zazen mixed with Taoism, Confucianism, the recitation of the *nembutsu*, or koan study. Rejecting them all, he became abbot of Tendo Monastery in Southern China and taught only zazen. He was the last of the great Chinese Zen masters. His teaching continues today thanks to Dogen, who carried it back with him to Japan in 1227.

O

Obaku (Ch., Huang-po, d. 850). Disciple of Hyakujo and master of Rinzai; one of the great masters of Tang China. His manner of teaching was often very rough and was widely imitated by his later successors in the Rinzai line. He is nevertheless held in the highest esteem by all masters, regardless of school or sect.

Okubo, Doshu. Renowned Dogen scholar, editor of *Dogen Zenji Zenshu* (*The Complete Works of Master Dogen*) (Tokyo: Shunjusha, 1930).

Oryoki, lit. "that which contains just enough." A set of nesting bowls used by Zen monks and nuns; the ceremonial use of these bowls during meals in a Zen monastery.

R

Rakusu. A small-sized kesa sewn from small pieces of cloth patched together in the style of a full kesa, about the size of a large envelope and worn hanging in front of the chest. As opposed to the kesa, the rakusu is not reserved for monks and nuns. Everyone who has received the bodhisattva (lay) ordination receives and wears it.

Rinzai School. Lineage founded by Master Rinzai Gigen (d. 866), whose origin dates back to seventh-century master Nangaku Ejo, a disciple of Eno (as was Seigen Gyoshi, source of the Soto lineage); one of the two great branches of Zen still alive today, along with Soto; emphasizes obtaining satori and using koans as a meditation tool.

Roshi, lit. *ro*, "old"; *shi*, "master." A respectful title traditionally used when a Zen master is of advanced age; currently also used by younger masters in the United States.

S

Samadhi (Jap., *zanmai*). State of meditation and open awareness during zazen; pure, unconscious concentration without object. Master Dogen said, "The *samadhi* of the buddhas and the patriarchs is frost and hail, wind and lightning."

Sampai (or *sanpai*), lit. "three prostrations." Three bows in rapid sequence from a standing position, going down first onto the knees, then touching the floor with the forehead. Feet, shins, knees, and forehead touch the ground, the bottom is tucked in, and the hands are raised slightly, palms upward. An act of respect, veneration, humility, and the dropping away of body and mind.

Samsara. The "wheel of life"; the cycle of existences (birth, death, rebirth) conditioned by attachment; opposite of nirvana.

Samu. Concentration on manual work for the benefit of a sangha, dojo, or temple, such as cooking, cleaning, etc.; work done without object, goal, or recompense; holy work.

Sandokai, lit. "Fusion of Difference and Sameness." Poem written by Chinese master Sekito Kisen in the eighth century; one of the founding texts of Zen, recited daily in Soto monasteries; cited and commented on by many masters. It is because the many proceed from the One that differences exist.

Sangha. Assembly of monks; community of disciples; one of the "Three Treasures" of Buddhism, along with Buddha and Dharma.

Sanshodoei. Collection of thirty short poems composed by Master Dogen. *Sansho* means "parasol pines" and was the former name of Mount Eihei in Japan.

Satori. Enlightenment or awakening produced by the fundamental cosmic power rather than by the ego; the actualization of *mushotoku*; not a special state of consciousness, but a return to the normal condition. In the Rinzai School, satori is the result of a successful practice and the object of a vehement quest; in the Soto School, practice itself is satori: in other words, fusion with the natural order of things.

Sawaki, Kodo (1880 – 1965). Revolutionary Soto master of twentieth-century Japan who made Zen teaching available to everyone, lay people and monastics alike; master of Taisen Deshimaru. He spent the latter part of his life traveling around Japan, teaching zazen in universities, town halls, and prisons, continuing in this manner until the mid-1960s when he could no longer walk. He never had his own temple and was called "Homeless Kodo."

Sekito Kisen (Ch., Shih-t'ou Hsi-ch'ien, 700 – 790). Disciple of Seigen and master of Yakusan; leading Chinese master of the golden Tang era. He always did zazen on a large stone – thus his name "Sekito," which means "stone-head." Author of the *Sandokai*.

Sensei, lit. "born earlier." Term of respectful endearment for a master in both Zen Buddhism and the martial arts. All close disciples of Master Deshimaru refer to him as "Sensei."

Sesshin, lit. "to touch the mind." Period, usually between two and ten days, when the sangha comes together for intense practice focusing on zazen and *samu*.

Seven Principles of Zen. Taisen Deshimaru was one of the few masters in the West who commented on Dogen's Seven Principles. They are:

1. *Shu sho ichi nyo* - Zazen and satori are one.
2. *Sho butsu ichi nyo* - All beings and Buddha are one.
3. *Shoden no buppo* - The true transmission of Buddhism
4. *Jijuyu zanmai* - The samadhi of zazen
5. *Kyo gyo sho itto* - Teaching, practice and satori are one.
6. *Butsu kojo no homon* - Beyond God or Buddha
7. *Shin jin ichi nyo* - Body and mind are one.

Shakyamuni (563 – 483 BCE), lit. "Silent Sage of the Shakaya Clan." The historical Prince Siddhartha Gautama, son of the King of Shakaya, a small kingdom in the Himalayan foothills of present-day Nepal. He left home at the age of twenty-nine, had his satori under the Bodhi tree at Bodh-Gaya at the age of thirty-five, and spent the rest of his life teaching his disciples. He died in the woods near the river Kushinagara at the age of eighty.

Shiho. Official transmission conferred by the master to the disciple, who is then authenticated as one of the successors of Buddha in that lineage.

Shikan (Kankei) (Ch., Kuan-chih Chih-hsien, d. 895). Chinese Dharma successor to Rinzai, who also studied under the nun Moshan Laoran.

Shikantaza, lit. "just sitting." The seated posture that encompasses the whole universe; does not use techniques such as breath-counting or koan study.

Shiki soku ze ku, ku soku ze shiki. "Form is emptiness, emptiness is form." *Shiki* is phenomena, thoughts, passions and physical matter; *ku* is the void, or the creative energy of the Cosmos. A quotation from the *Heart Sutra* (*Hannya Shingyo*) expressing the impermanence of all things, including emptiness itself.

Shin jin datsu raku, lit. "throwing down body and mind." Phrase pronounced by Master Nyojo during zazen and frequently repeated by Dogen in his writings. It perfectly describes what zazen practice is.

Shinjinmei. "Verses on Faith in Mind" by Master Sosan (d. 606), the third patriarch. One of the oldest Zen texts, revered by Rinzai and Soto schools alike. A collection of 73 two-line verses expressing the essence of Zen.

Shi shi kai. The closing lines of the *Gyohatsunenju* or Mealtime Sutra (known in the Deshimaru sangha as the Bussho Kapila). The quotation in full is: *Shi shi kai jiki kun, jiren ka fu ja shi, shin shin jin cho i hi, ki shu rin bu jo son.*

Shobogenzo, lit. "The Treasury of the Eye of the True Law." Master Dogen's main work, compiled in part by his disciple Ejo; the first great Buddhist text in Japanese; a dense work of inexhaustible wealth which recounts and develops all the teachings received in China by the founder of Japanese Soto Zen.

Shodoka, lit. "Song of Immediate Satori." Written by Chinese master Yoka Daishi in the eighth century; one of the four oldest Zen texts.

Shukke Kudoku, lit. "The Merits of Transcending Family Life." Chapter 86 of Dogen's *Shobogenzo*, in which he gives helpful and down-to-earth advice on leading the monastic life.

Shuzen. Stage-by-stage Zen practice which entails moving from one level of understanding to the next; usually associated with the Rinzai School and its different levels of koan study.

Sojiji. Along with Eiheiji, one of the two major training temples of the Japanese Soto School; founded by Master Keizan Jokin, one of Dogen's successors; located in Yokohama.

Sosan (Ch., Seng-Tsan, d. 606). Disciple of Eka, and thus the third patriarch. Author of the *Shinjinmei*, the first Zen text. He died while doing *kinhin*.

Sotapanna, lit. "he who has entered the current."

Soto-Rinzai mix (also called "Rinzoto" or "American mix"). Informal expression for the type of Zen practice introduced in the United States by Philip Kapleau and Hakuun Yasutani which combines elements of the Soto and Rinzai traditions.

Soto School. Zen school founded in ninth-century China by Master To-zan Ryokai (807 – 869) and his disciple Sozan Honjaku (840 – 901). The name "Soto" comes from the beginning characters of their names. Soto emphasizes *shikantaza*, simply sitting, rather than the koan practice essential to the Rinzai School. It was introduced to Japan by Dogen in 1227 upon his return from China. Kodo Sawaki, Taisen Deshimaru, and their successors are part of the Soto lineage.

Sozan Honjaku (840 – 901). Close disciple of Tozan Ryokai (807 – 869), whose teachings form the basis of the Soto School. Famous primarily for his development of the theory of the *Go-i*, the five stages or degrees of enlightenment.

T

Taigu (Koan) (Ch., Kao-an Ta-yü, ninth century). Disciple of Kisu Chijo in the Baso line; contemporary of Obaku and Rinzai; master of the nun Moshan, the first woman Dharma heir in the official Chan transmission.

Taiko. A senior monk or nun who has undergone at least five years' training; in Deshimaru's sangha, a term to identify one's elder in the practice.

Taoism. A generic word for Chinese folk religion/philosophy; at least as old as Buddhism and long present in China before Buddhism came there from India; expounded by the mythical *Lao-tse* in the *Tao Te King*, probably around the sixth century BCE. Its emphasis on the opposite principles of yin and yang and the flow of energy have been introduced to Westerners through Feng Shui, traditional Chinese medicine, and macrobiotic cooking.

Tathagata, lit. "the thus-gone one" or "thus-come one." One of the ten titles of the Buddha, which he himself used when speaking of himself or of other buddhas. Whether the sense "thus-gone" or "thus-come" is used makes for a basic difference between the Mahayana and the Hinayana traditions respectively.

Tendai. A school honoring the person of the Buddha, widespread in Japan. Its followers venerate Amitabha Buddha, whom they aspire to call upon at the hour of death.

Tenzo. Head cook in a Zen temple or monastery; one of the most important and challenging positions in the sangha.

Tokusan Senkan (Ch., Te-shan Hsuan-chien, 781 – 867). A scholar renowned for his knowledge of the *Diamond Sutra* who burned all his books to follow the Way and dedicate himself to the practice of zazen. Famous for his educational method named bokatsu, from bo, "stick" and katsu, "shout."

Tozan Ryokai (Ch., Tung-shan Liang-chieh, 807 – 869). Chinese master whose teachings, together with those of his disciple Sozan Honjaku (840 – 901), form the basis of the Soto School. Author of the *Hokyozanmai*, one of the founding Zen texts, still recited in Japanese monasteries.

Triple Treasure (or Three Treasures, Jap., *sambo*). The Buddha, the Dharma, and the Sangha.

U

Unmon Bunen (Ch., Yün-men Wen-yen, 864 – 949). Chan master, student of Seppo Gison and himself master of more than sixty Dharma successors. There exist many *mondos* and Zen koans concerning Unmon, who is perhaps most famous for his saying, "Every day is a good day."

W

Wanshi Shogaku (Ch., Hung-chih Cheng-chueh, 1091 – 1157). Chinese Soto master greatly admired by Dogen. Known for his pointed debates with Rinzai master Daie Soko on the advantage of Soto's "*mokusho* Zen" (silent sitting Zen) as compared to Rinzai's "*kanna* Zen" (spoken or koan Zen). Author of the *Zazenshin*, which was later adapted by Dogen in the *Shobogenzo*.

Z

Zafu. Round cushion used for sitting zazen. It is filled with kapok, a fiber from the seedpod of the Java Cotton tree, and modeled on the grass cushion on which Shakyamuni Buddha had satori.

Zagu. A small patchwork rectangle knelt upon by Zen monks and nuns during ceremonies, *mondos*, etc., to prevent the kesa from touching the ground.

Zazen. Zen meditation practice; sitting with legs crossed and back straight on a zafu, facing the wall (in the Soto tradition) or the center of the room (in the Rinzai tradition). Breathing is slow and deep, and the mind observes thoughts without following, judging, or rejecting them.

Zeisler, Mokusho Etienne (1946 – 1990). One of Master Deshimaru's closest disciples, who became a master in his own right and the first president of the Association Zen Internationale after Deshimaru's death in 1982.

Index
of Zen Stories

Other Titles of Interest
From Hohm Press

SIT
Zen Teachings of Master Taisen Deshimaru

edited by Philippe Coupey

"To understand oneself is to understand the universe."
—Master Taisen Deshimaru

Like spending a month in retreat with a great Zen master. SIT addresses the practice of meditation for both beginners and long-time students of Zen. Deshimaru's powerful and insightful approach is particularly suited to those who desire an experience of the rigorous Soto tradition in a form that is accessible to Westerners.

Paper, 375 pages, 18 b & w photographs, $19.95
ISBN: 0-934252-61-0

TO ORDER: Call 1-800-381-2700
or visit our website at www.hohmpress.com.

Zen Trash
The Irreverent and Sacred Teaching Stories of Lee Lozowick

Edited and with Commentary by Sylvan Incao

This book contains dozens of teaching stories from many world religious traditions— including Zen, Christianity, Tibetan Buddhism, Sufism and Hinduism — rendered with a twist of humor, irony or provocation by contemporary spiritual teacher Lee Lozowick. They are compiled from thirty years of Lozowick's talks and seminars in the U.S., Canada, Europe, Mexico and India.

Paper, 150 pages, $12. 95
ISBN: 1-890772-21-6

As It Is
A Year on the Road with a Tantric Teacher
by M. Young

A first-hand account of a one-year journey around the world in the company of a tantric teacher. This book catalogues the trials and wonders of day-to-day interactions between a teacher and his students, and presents a broad range of his teachings given in seminars from San Francisco, California to Rishikesh, India. As It Is considers the core principles of tantra, including non-duality, compassion (the Bodhisattva ideal), service to others, and transformation within daily life. Written as a narrative, this captivating book will appeal to practitioners of any spiritual path. Readers interested in a life of clarity, genuine creativity, wisdom and harmony will find this an invaluable resource.

Paper, 840 pages, 24 b&w photos, $29.95
ISBN: 0-934252-99-8

The Anti-Wisdom Manual

Ways and Means to Fail on the Spiritual Path

by Gilles Farcet, Ph.D.

Most spiritual books tell us what we should do, or how we should view things. *The Anti-Wisdom Manual* takes a different approach. It simply describes what people actually do to sabotage their own progress on the spiritual path, whatever their chosen way – Christian, Buddhist, Native American, Muslim, Jewish, or any other. Think of it as a handbook in reverse. Using humor and irony, while based in clarity and compassion, the author alerts readers to the common traps into which so many sincere seekers easily fall.

Paper, 176 pages, $14.95
ISBN: 1-890772-42-9

Halfway Up the Mountain

The Error of Premature Claims to Enlightenment

by Mariana Caplan
Foreword by Fleet Maull

Dozens of first-hand interviews with students, respected spiritual teachers and masters, together with broad research are synthesized here to assist readers in avoiding the pitfalls of the spiritual path. Topics include: mistaking mystical experience for enlightenment; ego inflation, power and corruption among spiritual leaders; the question of the need for a teacher, and disillusionment on the path. "Caplan's illuminating book...urges seekers to pay the price of traveling the hard road to true enlightenment." —*Publisher's Weekly*

Paper, 600 pages, $21.95
ISBN: 0-934252-91-2

Journey to Heavenly Mountain
An American's Pilgrimage to the Heart of Buddhism in Modern China
by Jay Martin

"I came to China to live in Buddhist monasteries and to revisit my soul," writes best-selling American author and distinguished scholar Jay Martin of his 1998 pilgrimage. This book is an account of one man's spiritual journey. His intention? To penetrate the soul of China and its wisdom. Anyone who has wondered about the health of monastic Buddhism in China today will find this a fascinating revelation. Anyone who longs for the serenity and clarity that the author sought will want to read this book. Well written and intelligent." – *Library Journal*

Paper; 263 pages; b&w photographs, $16.95
ISBN: 1-890772-17-8

You Have the Right to Remain Silent
Bringing Meditation to Life
by Rick Lewis

With sparkling clarity and humor, Rick Lewis explains exactly what meditation can offer to those who are ready to establish an island of sanity in the midst of an active life. This book is a comprehensive look at everything a beginner would need to start a meditation practice, including how to befriend an overactive mind and how to bring the fruits of meditation into all aspects of daily life. Experienced meditators will also find refreshing perspectives to both nourish and refine their practice.

Paper, 201 pages, $14.95
ISBN: 1-890772-23-2

Kishido
The Way of the Western Warrior
by Peter Hobart

The code of the samurai and the path of the knight-warrior—traditions from opposite sides of the globe—find a common ground in this book. In fifty short essays, Peter Hobart presents the wisdom, philosophy and teachings of the mysterious Master who first united the noble houses of East and West. Kishido prioritizes the ideals of duty, ethics, courtesy and chivalry, from whatever source they derive. This cross-cultural approach represents a return to time-honored principles from many traditions, and allows the modern reader from virtually any background to find the master within.

Paper, 130 pages, $12.95
ISBN: 1-890772-31-3

A Presence Behind the Lens
Photography and Reflections
by Nicholas Hlobeczy

This book features the exquisite photography of the author, whose work has been featured in exhibits around the U. S. Hlobeczy studied with Ansel Adams in 1961, and for fifteen years (1961-1976) with Minor White, one of America's master photographers. The book's photography is augmented by ten insightful essays about the nature of art and creativity, particularly highlighting the need for self-awareness, attunement to the "now" and other means of encouraging a sense of presence that allows us to see the things before us in essence, as they are.

Clothbound, 208 pages, 21+ b&w photographs, $29.95
ISBN: 1-890772-51-8

About the Author

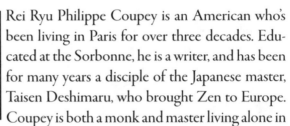

Rei Ryu Philippe Coupey is an American who's been living in Paris for over three decades. Educated at the Sorbonne, he is a writer, and has been for many years a disciple of the Japanese master, Taisen Deshimaru, who brought Zen to Europe. Coupey is both a monk and master living alone in the city, continuing the daily practice he was taught. He directs a large European community of monks and nuns. He is a member and officer of the International Zen Association AZI. His previous books include, *The Voice of the Valley*, and *SIT* (available through Hohm Press). His website is www.zen-road.org.